Successful Retirement

Published by Choice Publications Ltd
in conjunction with the
Pre-Retirement Association

Revised by Gill Crawley
and Jenny Harris
Design: Sharon Palmer
Illustrations: Robert Broomfield

GW00504248

Published by Choice Publications Ltd, Apex House,
Peterborough PE2 9NP
Printed in England

Successful Retirement

ISBN 0 906139 14 7

Fight cancer with a will

One day, we believe, a way will be found to defeat cancer. And if anyone is going to find the ultimate cure, it is the organisation which can concentrate its resources in a systematic and coordinated scientific approach.

We are the largest independent cancer research institute in Europe, employing over 1,000 scientists, doctors and technicians in our own laboratories and hospital units.

But we receive no state aid and depend entirely on the support and goodwill of the public.

Around 60% of our funds are raised by legacies and, thanks to our unique structure, over 90% of all donations are directly available for research.

So make your bequest to where you know it will do the most good. After all, where there's a will there's a way.

We would welcome your support.

Your bequest to us can take one of three forms:

i) the residue of your estate after full provision has been made for family and friends.

ii) a cash gift.

iii) an object of value.

The receipt of the Treasurer, Secretary or duly authorised Officer shall be good discharge for such legacy.

For further information please contact: The Legacy Department, Imperial Cancer Research Fund, PO Box 123, Lincoln's Inn Fields, London WC2A 3PX.

Imperial Cancer Research Fund

CONTENTS

Chapter one

INTRODUCTION

Make the most
of the good times ahead

It's a staggering thought. By the end of this century . . . just nine years from now . . . more than 40 per cent of the adult population will be aged 50 or over.

Already more than a third of the country's adults come into this category and this growing band look all set to be a real force to be reckoned with, at last seeing off the youth cult which has dominated everyone's lives for so long. To begin with they are likely to be much better off than previous generations.

By the time they reach 65 few will have to rely on the basic State Pension alone. Instead this will be supplemented by extra pensions from work.

In addition they will enjoy good health. Increased leisure means much more time for healthy exercise. On top of this are the sensible diets more and more families have already switched to and, just as important, a change of attitude.

What's more, the passing years won't be seen as disabling in any way . . . instead these over-50s will want to make the most of their maturity and increasing expertise. They will expect their opinions and experience to be valued, and in return they will be ready to face the new challenges ahead. Boredom and a dull life will certainly never be on the agenda.

MAKING IT WORK

Of course none of this will just happen overnight. And if you are about to enter this age group then making the most of the exciting times ahead will mean being quite sure about the money you have, the help you may be entitled to from the State as well as knowing how to get the most from your savings and what you should do to best look after your health.

Ever-changing rules and regulations often make modern living seem very confusing. It's all too easy, for instance, to miss out on something that is yours by right simply because the form you were asked to fill in didn't make sense. Knowing your rights is one thing, actually getting them is quite another.

Changes in interest rates, income tax and inflation can all make deciding what to do with any savings a real headache. Then there's the thought of possibly having to budget on a smaller income, as well as how to cope with the endless offers of financial "help" that you'll get the minute you retire.

That's where a very special magazine called CHOICE comes in. Each month its pages are packed with vital information on a host of different and important topics to help you cope.

And it's the magazine's special YOUR RIGHTS section which is bringing

you this useful guide, SUCCESSFUL RETIREMENT, to take you through your pension rights and other benefits, help you work out the income you will have to live on and show you the best ways to stay fit and on top form.

TIMING IT RIGHT

The key to a successful retirement is planning . . . and this guide will show you how, whether you have decided to work through till you are 65 or are considering, like so many others today, whether to go early.

It explains some of the important recent changes affecting pensioners, including all the 1991 Budget proposals.

In addition the book has at-a-glance tax tables, a section on State Benefits, your basic consumer and public rights plus lots of advice on how to stay in tip-top condition. What's more, the help and advice is based on the experience of the Pre-Retirement Association - experience which includes retirement preparation courses spanning everything from fitness to finance. So read on . . . you can be sure you are in good hands!

Chapter two

RETIRE NOW OR LATER

How to get your timing right

Working out when is the best time to retire isn't easy. If you have always hated your job you may want to go as soon as possible and will leap at any offers of early retirement.

The chances are you will want to do something else. It's a fact that a growing number of people don't ever actually retire. They may leave one job but they then start working part-time locally instead, or even get the business they have always dreamed about finally off the ground.

So it all depends on what you actually mean by retirement.

Traditionally women go at 60 and men at 65, but plenty of people carry on in the same jobs for another five years, just as many will start leaving much earlier at 55 or even 50.

But for the vast majority of people retirement still means giving up the job they have held for years and taking whatever State and employer's pension they are entitled to, perhaps working a little "on the side" to supplement what is probably a lower income.

At least the change in the Earnings Rule means they can now hang on to their earnings without their State Pension being affected.

Even so, before they can do this with any kind of confidence they need to be sure exactly what money they are going to be entitled to, as well as any benefits they may also be able to claim.

All this can make the difference between whether you should retire now or later. There are so many other things to consider too . . . those who are lucky enough to have a company car, for instance, will have to hand it back and this could mean having to buy one to replace it or investigating what kind of concessions - if any - are offered on local public transport.

CARRY ON EARNING

Since October 1989 when the Earnings Rule finally went you can earn what you want and claim your State Pension in full without it being affected once your money goes over a certain amount. This applies from the moment you reach official retirement age - still 60 for women and 65 for men.

This could be important if you plan to work for your old boss for a bit longer but in a different capacity, or even in the same job. DSS officials have yet to give clear guidance on this, but instead of putting off claiming your State Pension until you finally leave the company, you may be able to get that now and carry on working. This could be something worth investigating.

However, if you opt to carry on working in your present job for a further five years it may actually pay you not to claim your State Pension till you are 70 or, in the case of women, 65.

By officially deferring your State Pension - your company should be able to help you take this step - when you do finally get around to claiming it you'll actually get more in real terms, plus the periodic index-linked adjustments.

And you can change your mind. Once you decide to put off your pension like this you will not have to wait the full five years, if you suddenly changed your mind and decided you didn't want to carry on working after all - or if you fell ill.

But as soon as you let DSS officials know you plan to carry on working and earning, all the National Insurance contributions you have been making over the years start to work like an endowment.

The Government will increase your pension with inflation and, in addition, by a further 7.5% a year, making the deferred pension worth 37.5% more after the five years to age 70 (65 for women).

Experts regard endowments as remarkably tax-efficient - and the deferred pension is no exception. You pay no tax on it since you haven't actually benefited from it yet - and by the time you get around to it your "income" is likely to have been reduced sufficiently to ensure a minimal tax liability, or none at all.

To gain the maximum advantage of this deferrment you.should ask your employer for an Age Exemption Certificate which should be issued automatically once you tell the DSS you plan to carry on working.

This means you shouldn't have to make any more National Insurance contributions either and if your wages department continues to take this money out of your salary they will have to pay you back.

So is carrying on working a good idea? Only you can decide of course. But it can certainly make sense if your boss is willing to continue to employ you at the same wage and under the same conditions, you're in good health and your take-home pay is considerably higher than the basic State Pension.

Most experts reckon your wages should be at least twice the pension for it to be worthwhile.

Even if you can't stay in the same job or with the same employer it can still be worth deferring the State Pension provided you are sure you have sufficient income.

The rate of inflation is also important here. For although the extra pension is inflation linked, it is the net gain which makes it a bargain. And despite

MRS JONES' LIFE WAS DEVOTED TO TEACHING. SO WAS HER WILL.

After a lifetime of teaching Mrs. Jones might have felt she couldn't do much more to help the next generation. Instead she left a legacy of £16,000 to ActionAid. That money is being used for long term development of which education is an important part.

To give just one example, we're currently rebuilding schools torn apart (literally) by bandit attacks in Mozambique. This kind of help is vital in Africa and the rest of the Third World where commonly over half the population cannot read.

If like Mrs. Jones you feel that having provided for your family, you can still help the world's neediest people, we've produced a free booklet to help you make your will.

It explains the process and includes relevant legal forms, so you spend much less time with your solicitor and save money. A legacy allows you to give other people a place in your will – as well as in your life. Call this number or cut out the coupon and post it in an envelope **0460 62972** addressed to: ActionAid "Free Will Guide," Tapstone Road, Chard, Somerset TA20 2AB.

☐ Yes. Please send me the ActionAid "Making or Changing Your Will" pack.

I require details for: ☐ England, Wales, N. Ireland ☐ Scotland

Name

Address

Postcode   Tel.

90210

ActionAid

Tapstone Road, Chard, Somerset TA20 2AB. Registered charity number 274467.

15

index-linking high inflation still erodes your profit.

It's also worth noting that should anything happen to you, the increased pension would be paid to your widow or widower.

MAKING YOUR DECISION

So how can you decide what's best for you? One way is to write down all your options on a piece of paper. To do this properly you will have to finish reading this book of course - but if you have a notebook ready you can jot down the relevant bits as you go through the various sections.

And to help you work all this out there's a useful budget planner on page 76 you can fill in to help you make these calculations.

First of all list your present "income" . . . that's your earnings at work and from any investments or savings you may have. What would replace this if you gave up your job? You might get some company pension, for instance, but you could miss out here by claiming too early . . . see Chapter Four.

Then write down what your income would be at 60 or 65 if you retire at the "official" time. Last but not least calculate what you would happen if you put off your retirement till you were 65 or 70.

To help you make these calculations the DSS now offers a special forecasting service about what State Pension you will get depending on exactly when you decide to retire. Ask for Form BR19.

At first glance the form you are asked to fill in does look a bit complicated but in fact it is very straightforward - though the reply you get back may not be!

Once you have a clear picture of the money situation you need to work out your outgoings - and whether these will change once you stop working. Heating costs will increase, for example, if you are home more but you may well save on food and travel costs.

And this may be just as true if you decide to take some kind of part-time job locally - in fact you might find you are actually better off than now simply because your outgoings are so much less even though your earnings are reduced.

Only when you have worked all this out can you make your final decision.

But the most important point of all is that it should be your choice when you finally decide to retire. At the end of the day it is much better to retire voluntarily than to feel forced in some way.

Switching to something else is likely to offer you a real challenge - after all, a change is as good as a rest. But if this is what you decide to do then you will need to start planning now - you don't suddenly want to find yourself

in a position where you don't have any options.

On the other hand it's also a fact that many retired people carry on putting away lots of money "for a rainy day" when in fact they could be enjoying some of it now. What matters is to get the balance right.

Once you have worked out your cash situation for all the choices open to you, then you want to make sure too that there will be no chance of boredom and loneliness ruining any of your ideas. The secret is to be realistic about just what will replace the hours of work you have been putting in every day.

Plan meticulously for the better things in life . . . you deserve them! Then put in your notice at whatever age you finally decide to call it a day, making sure that you have a very good idea about just how you are going to be spending all that wonderful free time you will have on your hands!

Chapter three

EARLY RETIREMENT

Facts to help you choose

These days going early is an option more and more people are deciding to take. One reason is that they are much better off than previous generations, but in addition they have a very different attitude.

Today life is to be enjoyed and for more and more of us that does not mean sitting in a long traffic jam on the way to work every day or fighting for a seat on the train.

By 50 or so, lots of us are beginning to get tired of all this hassle. If you are in this age group you may well have finished paying off your mortgage - and even if you haven't, your house will be worth a lot more than it was when you first bought it.

You may have inherited a bit of money or made one or two good investments. And on top of all this you could have put sufficient into your company pension fund to get a decent sum.

All these things may well make you decide to launch into something new. It's worth noting that there are now loans, Government grants and finance available if a business of your own is your "retirement" plan.

It's a fact of course that as an employee you may well have been cotton-woolled against the harder facts of business life. You will probably have had few direct dealings with the tax man. Your salary cheque arrives on time each month.

Take the plunge to become self-employed and all this will change - and often not entirely for the better, certainly to begin with anyway. You need to budget for this carefully - and get expert help.

All the major High Street banks now have active small business sections which not only advise and lend in their own right, but can also give you details of a very wide range of other grants.

Remember, though, that if you are not impressed with your own particular branch you have the right to change banks. Today's competition among the big banks is pretty cut-throat and shopping around can really pay.

WHEN THERE'S NO CHOICE

For some early retirers it isn't choice that makes them go . . . it's redundancy. There's no doubt that to be made redundant at 50 or 55 after a lifetime of loyal service can be a catastrophic experience. But for lots of people it really is a new beginning - and years later they are pleased it happened.

All the evidence shows that many people made redundant after a long period of service do much better afterwards than they ever did in their traditional workplace.

However, in a situation like this it's important to take advice - from your firm's counsellors, for example, who in any large-scale redundancy programme will be called in to help you.

If you find yourself in this situation, much will depend of course on the size of any redundancy payment you get. As a rule it will be based on the number of years service you have put in . . . certainly this is the case for the minimum State provision.

Provided you meet the qualifying conditions - you must have been with the company for two years, for instance, and work a certain number of hours each week - then as a rough guide you get a minimum of one and a half times current weekly pay up to a maximum of £198 for each year worked after 18, to a maximum of 20 years.

Some part-time workers may be eligible if they have been with the company for five years or more.

The current maximum statutory redundancy payment is about £5,940.

Lots of people will get less than this, of course. More generous amounts are more likely from packages worked out between bosses and workers - perhaps when new technology comes in. Then you are more likely to get the kind of nest-egg that you can really do something with.

You don't have to pay tax until the payment reaches £30,000. But however much you get the most important step you can take is not to do anything until you have got expert help.

If your company hasn't brought in anyone to help you here then you must make sure the kind of advice you get is independent. Your Citizens Advice Bureau - address in the phone book - is a good starting point. Or you could try the IFA Promotion Ltd helpline on O81-200 3000. The IFA stands for Independent Financial Advisers and if you phone the helpline you'll be given a list of 10 registered advisers in your area.

In the meantime put the money somewhere safe and don't touch it till you are quite sure you know what your plans are.

It's also important to sign on at your Unemployment Benefit Office, not just to draw any Unemployment Benefit that you are entitled to but also to help safeguard your State Retirement Pension for the future. While you claim Unemployment Benefit your National Insurance contributions that go towards your State Pension are credited and you won't miss out.

Then you will have to look for another job. And it may be that instead of going to work for another employer you decide to use your redundancy pay to set up something on your own.

It's a fact that lots of the most successful small businesses in recent years have been founded on redundancy.

YOUR PENSION ENTITLEMENT

Lots of people who want to retire early get confused about what pension they will get. The answer is that regardless of what your private pension arrangements are, early retirement does not entitle you to the State Pension yet.

You will not be able to claim this until you reach the official pension age of 65 for a man and 60 for a woman. And you would need to check the situation regarding contributions should you retire earlier than this, to make sure you could still get the full amount when you reach the "official" age.

Remember, an occupational pension scheme counts as income and can adversely affect whatever Unemployment Benefit you might receive. Others may be forced to retire early through ill-health when they will get Sickness rather than Unemployment Benefit. This is payable right away and, unlike Unemployment Benefit, is tax-free.

The tax rules on occupational pension schemes or company pensions have become more complicated in recent years, but the 1989 Budget may have helped some of those who wanted to retire early.

Basically, what happened then was that the relief given to the self-employed which allowed them to take their personal pension savings at any age after 50 was, in part, extended to employees. A maximum of two-thirds final salary may now be paid in pension on retirement between 50 and 70, though to qualify you must have been with the same employer for 20 years.

But the reality is probably nowhere near as generous and will depend on individual schemes and their provisions.

There have also been changes to the tax-free lump sum provision within some company schemes. This means you can now sometimes take a lump sum of up to one and a half times your final salary.

Should you be among that very small percentage of workers on an income of £71,400 a year or more, that £71,400 is where tax relief stops both for personal and occupational pensions.

But the calculations are complicated. The maximum tax-free lump sum for occupational pension schemes is currently defined as either 3/80 of final salary or 2.25 times the amount of pension before commutation, whichever is better. But there's always an overall limit that means you can't get over one and a half times final pay in either case.

What this could mean in some cases is more cash is available to you at a younger age when you can probably put it to better use - setting up a business, for instance. But not every scheme offers this chance of course.

All this makes early retirement dependent on the rules of your company scheme . . . or how much you have managed to put into your personal pension.

Government regulations mean you can't have a refund from previous employers' schemes after you have put in two years' pensionable service.

SAFEGUARDING YOUR LIFESTYLE

There's one thing anyone retiring early will soon notice - the major difference between work and retirement is the end of those annual rises which kept you at least in step with inflation.

Once you are retired you will be very much at the mercy of inflation. Even though your State Pension is index-linked and will rise each year, this rise is linked to the previous year's inflation rate so you will always be one step behind.

In addition an occupational pension, based as it is on what the employer is prepared to provide, is far less likely to be fully index-linked and may become less in real terms the longer you draw it. And the earlier you start the sooner you are likely to notice this.

You need to get good independent financial advice on how best to

BLIND SHE MAY BE BUT HER LIFE IS NOT WITHOUT VISION

Along with many other visually handicapped youngsters of all ages Daniella is being taught at Dorton House School to cope with her disability and achieve a remarkable degree of independence.

Such is the demand for places at Dorton House that The Royal London Society for the Blind has an ambitious £1.8m expansion programme but we rely entirely on private funding to implement it.

Will you express your gratitude for the gift of sight by sending a donation and mentioning us in your Will? So that Daniella, without sight, need not be without vision.

To: Peter Driver, The Royal London Society for the Blind
105 Salusbury Road, London NW6 6RH

I enclose   £10 ☐   £25 ☐   £50 ☐   £100 ☐   £ ☐

Please debit my credit card for £ _____ by   [ACCESS] [VISA] [DINERS] [AMERICAN EXPRESS]

Account Number ☐☐☐☐☐☐☐☐☐☐☐☐☐☐☐☐

Name _____ Signature _____ Date _____

Address _____

_____ Postcode _____   SR91

TO DONATE BY PHONE PLEASE RING
OUR DIRECT LINE 071 372 1807

Patron: Her Majesty The Queen   President: H.R.H. The Duchess of Gloucester   Registered Charity No. 307892

ROYAL
LONDON
SOCIETY for the
BLIND

25

safeguard your position. There are some new Government schemes worth investigating - you could consider putting some of your money into TESSA, a five year bank or building society investment where you pay no tax if capital remains untouched but you can draw out the interest.

There's more about all this in the "Your Savings" chapter. But whatever you do, try to resist the understandable temptation to pay off all your financial obligations and then live on basic income.

Instead, make what money you have work actively for you in retirement since you will have fewer chances of making additional income - and this can apply even if you take this step early.

If you are going to take on another job, fair enough, but if not you must bear this in mind.

SHOULD YOU PAY UP?

And what about paying off your mortgage? Using redundancy money for this could well be a mistake, especially if you then start working again. For a start you get basic rate tax relief on the interest on repayments up to £30,000.

However, if you are retiring nearer the "official" age and not planning to carry on working more than part-time, using a pension lump sum to pay off your mortgage can sometimes make sense.

The answer depends on the mortgage interest rate in force at the time. High mortgage interest rates, despite tax relief, make it more difficult to find alternative investments which will earn enough to cover the cost of the interest you are paying.

In this situation paying off can be the answer, but this is an area where you should get expert advice.

Another idea is to use any lump sum you get to improve the house, looking particularly to those grant-aided improvements, such as for certain types of insulation, which will both cut fuel bills in the future and increase the price you will get for the property should you sell up later.

One area potential early-retirers should look at carefully is the increased proportion of earnings they can put tax-free into special savings schemes like personal pensions. Anyone aged between 46 and 50 can use 25% of income, while those aged 51 to 55 can use 30%. Above that age 35% can go to a personal plan with full tax relief and at 61 and over, 40%.

All this is good news for someone going self-employed and earning enough to afford the contributions. You can lose over a third of what you make net, subject to a ceiling few of us are likely to reach at £71,400.

Chapter four

YOUR PENSION EXPLAINED

Working out what
you are entitled to

Provided you have paid enough National Insurance contributions then at the very least you will be entitled to the full basic State Pension paid at 60 to women and at 65 to men.

"Enough" means you have been making full contributions for at least nine-tenths of your working life, that is 40 years for women and 44 for men.

Every week you are at work your employer makes contributions on your behalf and you may be credited for any you miss in certain circumstances - perhaps because you are unemployed, for instance.

Even if you don't qualify for a full pension, you may well be entitled to a scaled-down one.

It's only if you have not managed to notch up contributions for at least ten years that you won't be eligible for any at all.

Most of those retiring in this position will be women who spent many years at home bringing up children or looking after dependants.

Since 1978 women in this situation have been able to claim Home Responsibilities Protection so they can be credited for these years. However, as this protection is not allowed to be backdated it has come too late to help most of those retiring now.

WHAT YOU WILL GET

So how do you find out what you will get? You can do this quite easily now by contacting the DSS special Retirement Pensions Forecasting Advice Unit in Newcastle.

As well as the basic State Pension you can expect, the Forecasting Unit can also tell you of any additional pension you might be entitled to plus any Graduated Retirement Benefit based on the old graduated scheme which ran from 1961 to 1976.

Depending on what you paid then, you could get a few pounds extra each week on top of your basic State Pension.

The other scheme you may get something from is called SERPS or the State Earnings Related Pension Scheme.

If you are in a pension scheme at work the chances are you will be contracted out of this, but not necessarily.

Some company schemes pay out a pension on top and the forecasting unit will be able to tell you if you are eligible for any SERPS benefit.

FINDING OUT

The key to finding all this out is filling in the special form correctly. You need form BRl9 from your local DSS office. Phone and get them to send it

The sign on the building reads:

DHSS
STATE PENSION
FORECAST
DEPT.

to you if that's easier - if you don't know the number look in the phone book under "health & social security" or just "social security".

The secret is to give all the information asked for when you can, even if some of the questions seem a bit unnecessary. The form doesn't always explain the logic behind each question . . .

On the other hand don't worry if you can't answer them all - you might not be able to remember your National Insurance number, for instance. The DSS can usually trace this through your name and date of birth. Otherwise they may ask you to check with your last employer.

Alternatively they may start a search through their local office - but then officials need to know if you have ever changed your name. The form will ask you this and it pays to give all the surnames you have ever had including, in the case of a woman, her maiden name.

There are also questions about divorce.

The chief reason for this is the rule that allows any gaps in the National Insurance contribution record to be filled from the other partner's record where possible. And this is allowed until the end of the tax year in which the divorce takes place.

It makes no difference to the other person, who probably won't even know.

Anyone expecting to get divorced within the current tax year gets two forecasts in fact - one on the assumption that they will still be married and the other assuming that the divorce has gone through.

What if a couple are separated? Well, until you actually get a divorce you are treated as still married for pension purposes.

CONTRIBUTION CREDITS

You will also be expected to answer questions about any benefits you are claiming - you may then be entitled to some sort of credit for the contributions you aren't making, because you are currently claiming Unemployment Benefit, for instance.

In this same section there are extra questions about Child Benefit. The person whose name appears above the address on the cover of the book is regarded as the "main payee".

This entitles them to the Home Responsibilities Protection mentioned before, in case looking after their children has meant a gap in their National Insurance contribution record because they haven't gone out to work. That way their State Pension is protected for that time.

You may also be entitled to credits if you have lived abroad. If there was some sort of reciprocal agreement with that particular country your contribution record is more likely to be up to date.

Common Market countries have these special arrangements, as do some Commonwealth ones.

WHICH RATE?

But whatever the forecast reveals there is a chance you could make up some of the missing contributions . . . or take advantage of some of the more recent changes to the way the contributions system now works.

Since October 1989, for example, women on low wages who elected to pay the special "married woman's stamp" when it was on offer - which ruled out a State Pension of their own - could find they would now get a better deal if they switched to paying the full contribution.

National Insurance contributions are earnings-related but what has changed is the way this is calculated and those earning less than, say, £60 a week could find they would actually be paying less on the full rate.

But it's worth remembering that once a woman makes the switch there is no going back, so before opting to "switch" in this way she would have to be sure it was the right thing and her wages were not suddenly going to increase dramatically, resulting in a larger National Insurance Contribution.

She would need to check out the switch carefully to see if there was still time for her to benefit with her own pension and this is where her official forecast should be able to help.

MAKING UP FOR LOST TIME

Anyone who has had an interrupted working life could find it would be worth their while making up for any lost contributions by paying for those missing years now. You are only allowed this voluntary back-dating for lapses in the last six years - in other words you can't go back further than, say, 1985 and you can only do this before retirement. Once women reach 60 and men 65, it's too late.

If you ask, officials can show you in your forecast what would happen if you did decide to make up any "lost" contributions like this.

After all this, the basic State Pension isn't large - currently £52 a week from this April if you are single and £31.25 for a dependant. As far as the graduated scheme is concerned the most you can get is £5.45 a week if you're a man and £4.55 if you're a woman.

Worth noting - a woman who paid into this scheme can claim even if she's not entitled to a basic State Pension because of her contribution record. So, even if she's waiting for her husband to retire, she can still get something.

PENSIONS FROM JOBS

Because you get full tax relief on contributions made into an approved pension scheme, there's a top limit on what any company pension scheme can give you. Basically, the most pension you will be able to get from your employers is two-thirds of what you were earning just before retirement.

The majority of pensions schemes are "contracted out" of the State Earnings Related Pension Scheme (SERPS). You get an ordinary basic State Pension based on your contribution record, but if your scheme has been contracted out then the extra pension you get comes from your employer rather than the State.

Most good employers will keep you informed by giving out annual statements about how your pension is building up. You have the right under the Disclosure of Information Regulations 1986 to insist that they do.

Details of your scheme's benefits are often in a booklet handed out to all members. The law actually says these booklets should be kept up to date, but that doesn't always happen in reality. If it's a while since yours was updated, it is worth double checking that nothing has changed.

On the booklet there will be an address where you can write if you want more information.

There are several sorts of pension schemes, but most employer-run schemes are of the sort called "final earnings". With these the pension is worked out according to a set formula. But the exact definitions can make a big difference.

You might find your scheme gives a pension based on all your earnings in the last year before you retire. Others take account only of basic earnings, without making any allowance for overtime or commission.

What's regarded as "pensionable service" also varies from one occupational pensiion scheme to another.

Sometimes you have to put in a couple of years' work before you are allowed to join and, depending on the rules of your employer's scheme, this time may or may not count in the final calculations.

With some schemes, you may be given the opportunity to "buy" the extra years.

That's why it would pay you to go through the small print of your booklet to see exactly what you're going to get - and there's nothing to stop you trying to get the scheme improved. There may be a special committee you can approach or you could ask your trade union for help.

INFLATION-PROOFING

Before retiring you should check how much pension your company will pay you and how far it is inflation-proof. Employees in the public sector like the Civil Service, local authorities, NHS and teachers will get inflation-proof pensions automatically. But employees in the private sector may get little inflation-proofing built in.

As from January 1 1991 pensions based on final salaries must be inflation-proofed to 5% or in line with the Retail Price Index, whichever is the lower.

But some companies will only increase pensions based on service AFTER that date, which won't help people who are retiring in the near future, while others are accepting the spirit of the law and, if there is enough money in the pension fund, are applying the increases to all previous service. Ask your pension administrators what their policy is.

If you have changed jobs you may have left some pension rights behind and may have lost track of them. If so, the Registry of Pension Schemes, a new body, may be able to help. The address is PO Box 1NN, Newcastle upon Tyne, NE99 1NN. Tel: 091 225 6393.

Lump sum payments

It is possible to sometimes give up part of your pension in return for a one-off lump sum payment. In official jargon this is called "commuting" your pension. As a rough guide, a man aged 65 could get a cash sum of £900 for every £100 a year of pension he gives up, whereas a woman of 60 might get £1,100 as statistically she is expected to draw her pension for longer. But this difference doesn't always apply, it depends on the particular scheme.

The most you can have in a lump sum is one and a half times your current earnings but most people get a lot less than this.

Many people find the option of commuting an attractive one, as it gives them a lump sum to invest as s comforting nest-egg for the future or spend on something specific - like that once-in-a-lifetime holiday they've always promised themselves. Only you can decide whether commuting is a good idea, depending on your personal circumstances.

If you have to retire early because of ill health, you are unlikely to be penalised - in fact some schemes are boosted for the sick.

Otherwise going early is likely to cost you as, understandably, the longer you are likely to receive a pension, the more the money you put in has to be stretched.

Avcs

If you find your pension isn't going to be as good as you had hoped you can add benefits to it yourself by paying what are called Additional Voluntary Contributions or AVCs.

Every employer's scheme must now offer to take AVCs and invest them on an employee's behalf, but if you prefer you can pay AVCs to an outside investment firm, though you are unlikely to get such good value because you have to pay something for setting it up.

You can pay up to 15% of your earnings in any one tax year towards your pension as your own contribution and get full tax relief. In other words, if 5% of your earnings are currently going into the main scheme, you could add an extra 10% in AVCs.

While the most you can have as a pension is still two-thirds of your final earnings, so long as you have been in the scheme for at least 20 years the good news is you can take this maximum pension at any age from 50 upwards. But in reality the amount you get is likely to be a lot less

How to complain

A new Pensions Ombudsman has been appointed to deal with individual complaints. He is Michael Platt and he will work in conjunction with the Occupational Pensions Advisory Service, a voluntary outfit which offers advice to individuals. Contact OPAS at 8a Bloomsbury Square, London, WC1A 2UA. Tel: 071 233 8080.

Chapter five

State benefits and your rights

A guide to your entitlements

It's a sad fact that many pensioners do find it extra hard to make ends meet, but there are benefits they could be entitled to which can help.

The most important point to remember is that they have been paid for through National Insurance contributions over the years - and the benefits are the right of those entitled to them. This is not charity and it's essential to know just what is available and who can claim it.

INCOME SUPPORT

This replaced the old Supplementary Benefit. To qualify your savings must be £8,000 or less and neither you nor your partner should work for 24 hours a week or more.

To calculate whether or not you are then entitled to the benefit you must first add up all your savings, apart from the value of your home, and the surrender value of your life insurance policy. If these total more than £3,000, the benefit will be gradually scaled down by £1 per £250 of savings to a cut-off limit of £8,000 when Income Support ceases.

Next you must list your weekly income - that's all the money coming to you after tax and National Insurance have been paid. For these calculations you don't need to include some other benefits you might be claiming such as Housing Benefit, Mobility or Attendance Allowance or income from savings below the £8,000 limit.

But you would need to check all this out very carefully with the DSS - it is complicated. For instance, if you let out a room in your house, how much of the rent you can discount depends on whether heating costs are included in the rent or not.

What money you actually get depends on the sum the DSS calculates you need to live on each week. If you have less than this sum you can claim Income Support to make up the difference.

All this is explained in booklet IS20, A Guide to Income Support, from the DSS - if you need help filling the claim form in, your Citizens Advice Bureau (address in the phone book) or Welfare Rights Agency are a good bet. As a rule, this benefit would be added to your retirement pension and paid out with it.

SOCIAL FUND

What this does is provide cash for a variety of one-off payments from cold weather help to funeral costs. Someone responsible for the costs of a funeral who is already on Income Support or Housing Benefit would be eligible to apply for one of these grants. But if they or the deceased had any savings (£500 for under 60, £1,000 for over) this would be taken into account and any grant adjusted accordingly.

Again, pensioners claiming Income Support may be entitled to extra help to meet the costs of fuel during very cold weather through this particular fund.

Provided any savings are less than £500 (£1,000 if over 60) a claim can be made for any seven-day period when the average temperature is O degrees Centigrade or below.

The £500 or £1,000 savings barrier applies to all discretionary payments your local DSS office can advance you from the Social Fund and should not be confused with the £3,000 to £8,000 savings limit for Income Support.

But the most important point about grants from the Social Fund is that some of them are loans,while others do not need paying back. The one thing they all have in common is that they are discretionary - in other words what one person may get in Yorkshire another in exactly the same situation in Lancashire may not.

See Guide to the Social Fund, Booklet SB16, available from the DSS.

COMMUNITY CARE GRANT

These grants do not have to be repaid. They are available to certain high priority groups of people on Income Support, including elderly people with restricted mobility as well as the handicapped.

You can get a grant to help with moving from institutional or residential care back into the community to cover such things as bedding, cookers, fuel connections, removal charges and so on.

Community Care Grants are also available to help someone avoid going into care by paying for "essentials" like furniture and minor household repairs and for families under pressure facing disability, chronic sickness or breakdown of marriage.

Finally, you can get a Community Care Grant to help with urgent and often unexpected travel expenses, such as visiting someone in hospital or attending a close relative's funeral.

WHEN IT'S ONLY A LOAN

The other payments made through the Social Fund are only loans. Again, they are only granted at the Social Fund Officer's discretion and must be repaid within 78 weeks or 18 months. Normally this is done by deducting what you owe from your other regular benefit payments.

Though the loans are discretionary, the Social Fund Officer works within a legal framework and according to a defined set of rules, but to a strictly limited budget for his area. Once this budget has been used up there is literally no more money available for applicants to the fund. This is the main reason why the loans are not yours by right.

There are basically two types of loan, so you need to be clear which type you are entitled to and which covers your needs.

The first are BUDGET LOANS which are restricted to those who have been on Income Support for at least 26 weeks and need essential items they could not otherwise afford.

The Social Fund Officer is expected to give priority to applications for such basics as bedding, clothing and moving costs and not "luxury" items like a TV set, for example. But in poorer areas where the demands on the Fund are greatest, the cash limits mean you may be refused a loan even for something deemed an essential item.

The loan will be deducted at a rate of between 5% and 15% from your Income Support, for up to 18 months.

It's important to take into account the cost of repayment. The loans are interest-free but repayments will still make a hole in your Income Support.

CRISIS LOANS are different because they are not restricted to people on Income Support. As their name suggests, they are for emergencies such as fire or flood or if the cooker breaks down, and other situations where your health or safety have been put at serious risk.

Again, they are only granted at the discretion of the Social Fund Office, which will take into account your savings and income, the size of the loan and the period over which you must repay it. But most important, the office will also check out whether the cash help is available from any other sources - local government for example, or charity.

HOW TO CLAIM

You apply for either a loan or a grant on claim form SF300 available from your local DSS office. Try to include as much additional information as possible, even if you put it on an extra sheet of paper.

Obviously, the grant offers a much better deal than a loan which is why it can be worth enlisting some expert help with filling in the form. Try your Citizens Advice Bureau (address in the phone book) which will have people used to dealing with these forms.

If you are turned down then your right of appeal is limited and the final decision rests with the Department of Social Security whose officer refused you the money in the first place.

HOUSING BENEFIT

This is an important benefit for those on low incomes - it's basically non-taxable help with rent for those on a very tight budget.

Housing Benefit, also called rent rebate or rent allowance, is administered by the local authority under rules drafted by the Government.

People in private residential or nursing homes can also sometimes get help with the rent part of their costs provided they are not on Income Support. But Housing Benefit cannot be given to people in a local authority home.

WORKING IT OUT

If the kind of accommodation you have is specially geared up for the elderly and the rent includes service charges for such things as cleaning, portering, caretaking and rubbish removal and the cost of the emergency alarm system, then the maximum benefit you could claim is 100%.

To see if you may be eligible, the first step is to calculate your weekly rent. If you have other people sharing your home with you, you can deduct a certain amount from these figures for people other than your partner aged 18 and over who live in your home. How much you deduct depends on the age and circumstances of the person concerned.

The next step is to add up the value of your savings, including cash, bank, building society and National Savings Accounts, National Savings Certificates, Premium Bonds, stocks and shares and half of any joint savings you may have with someone else. For a couple you take both your savings but the following exclusion limits remain the same for both couples and single people: savings of £3,000 or less are discounted but between £3,000 and £16,000 will affect the benefit.

You must then add up your weekly income to a set formula - you are allowed to ignore some benefits, for instance. And if it is the same or less than the Government figure for what you need you may well be entitled to have all your rent paid.

COMMUNITY CHARGE BENEFIT

The 1991 Budget announced the forthcoming abolition of the Community Charge from 1993/4. A new system of local government finance, possibly linked to a property tax (taking into account the value of the property and the number of people living there), will be introduced. A change of government before then could mean yet another change in the way local taxation is collected! In the meantime an adapted form of the Community Charge remains in place.

First of all, everybody's 1991-92 poll tax bill will be cut by £140. Next, a more generous Community Charge Reduction Scheme, which replaces Transitional Relief from April 1991, helps ratepayers facing increases which are too high. This is not means tested and goes automatically to people who qualify.

Some pensioners and disabled people who were non-ratepayers before all this controversy erupted can get extra Community Charge reduction by applying to their council.

Even after the £140 is lopped off and the Community Charge Reduction Scheme are taken into account, people with no more than £16,000 in savings and on a low income may still be entitled to Community Charge Benefit.

If you are claiming Housing Benefit then it's likely the council has sent you a claim form for a rebate.

If you don't agree with the council's assessment, you have the right to appeal. First you can ask officials to take another look at their calculations, but if you still aren't satisfied then you can ask to have the decision reviewed by a local review board.

Age Concern publishes a free information sheet called The Comunity Charge (Poll Tax) and Older People, available on receipt of a large SAE, from Age Concern England, 1268 London Road, London, SW16 4ER.

INVALIDITY BENEFIT

Invalidity Benefit is not taxable and is paid to people who have been unable to work for at least 28 weeks due to ill health. It is paid at the same rate as the basic State Retirement Pension. Where it scores over the ordinary pension is that it is tax-free and is therefore not affected by savings or any other income.

In other words the basic Invalidity Benefit is worth more than the identical State Pension to the taxpayer and can, of course, be paid well before the normal retirement age.

While this is of little consolation to the victim, those who become unable to work more than five years before official retirement age (65 for men, 60 for women) are also entitled to an extra weekly sum, the Invalidity Allowance.

The rules governing this are a bit complicated because there are three rates at which the allowance is paid, depending on the age at which you became unable to work. From April 1991 for those under 40 it is £11.10, between 40 and 49, £6.90 and for men aged 50 to 59 and women aged 50 to 54, £3.45. These sums are paid in addition to the Invalidity Benefit, subject to certain conditions.

If you are also entitled to an additional Invalidity Benefit on earnings on which you paid Class 1 National Insurance contributions from 1978, your money will either be topped up or cut back to the level of the additional allowance. In other words, you cannot claim double benefit.

For instance, somebody entitled to the £3.45 Invalidity Allowance on top of his or her £52 Invalidity Benefit may also be drawing an additional pension of £2 a week. The Invalidity Allowance would then only be 20p.

Someone who becomes eligible for Invalidity Benefit after the 28 weeks of being unable to work can also claim the dependant adult addition of £31.25 a week for their partner though their income - including any occupational pension - must fall below a certain figure.

Any work someone on this benefit does must be undertaken for therapeutic reasons only on doctor's advice and earnings must be under £41.40 a week.

At age 60 for women and 65 for men all this changes.

You can then opt to draw the State Pension while still getting the Invalidity Allowance or continue with full Invalidity Benefit until age 70 (65 for women) when you will have to go on to any State Pension to which you are entitled.

Before deciding which to go for, remember that Invalidity Benefit is not taxable whereas the State Pension plus Invalidity Allowance paid with it is. Invalidity Benefit may also entitle you to a higher level of Income Support than you would get with the State Pension.

Claiming Invalidity Benefit takes no effort on your part.

It is automatic after the 28 weeks on Sickness Benefit or Statutory Sickness Pay anyone at work gets when they fall ill. However, you will have to see that sick certificates are sent regularly from your doctor.

SEVERE DISABLEMENT ALLOWANCE

This is for very disabled people whose condition is sufficiently serious to prevent them working but who have not paid enough National Insurance contributions to be entitled to Invalidity Benefit.

The Severe Disablement Allowance is currently worth £31.25 a week.

You must have been unable to work for at least 28 weeks and be below pension age when you apply for this allowance, as well as having been resident in the UK for 10 out of the previous 20 years.

Your particular disability will be assessed on a percentage scale according to a rather complicated set of rules and you must be what's officially termed 80% disabled or getting other benefits such as Mobility or Attendance Allowance.

You are not allowed to draw a retirement pension and the allowance as well - but should you not qualify for the pension or if the pension you do get is less than the £31.25 a week, you can continue on the higher figure and not "retire".

MOBILITY ALLOWANCE

The Mobility Allowance of £29.10 a week is for disabled people who have great difficulty in walking or who cannot walk at all. It is not taxable and neither depends on National Insurance contributions, nor is subject to any savings or earnings limits.

The other important point is that drawing it does not affect your other pension or benefits. In other words, once you meet the qualifying conditions, this is yours by right and nothing else you claim is affected.

You qualify if you have become fully or virtually unable to walk through a physical disability before the age of 65 (for both men and women in this case). This problem must be likely to remain for at least a year. You must also have been living in the UK for a year out of the previous 18 months.

The claim must be in at the latest by your 66th birthday and for those who still qualify can continue to be claimed up to the age of 80.

Claimants get some other incorporated benefits too. Someone on the Allowance who is still able to drive a car in some form does not need to pay any Road Tax. If someone else uses a car mostly to meet their needs - a son or daughter perhaps - then they, too, can claim Road Tax Exemption.

Claimants can also apply to the local council to join the Orange Badge Scheme for which there is sometimes a small charge, but this varies from area to area. This allows free parking in certain restricted areas. This concession is also available to another driver using the car mainly on their behalf.

To claim Mobility Allowance contact your local DSS office who will arrange a special medical examination on which they will base their decision whether to grant it.

Since there have been several well publicised and controversial cases where this allowance has been refused, do get expert advice from your local Citizens Advice Bureau in the event of any appeal.

INVALID CARE ALLOWANCE

This allowance is not made to the disabled person himself but to those under pensionable age who are unable to work because they are caring for a disabled person. The disabled person they are looking after does not necessarily have to be a relative or even live in the same house. The allowance is currently £31.25.

There is an additional allowance for a dependant adult and another for a dependant child.

This benefit does not depend on National Insurance contributions, but the person being cared for must be getting Attendance Allowance or similar. And the person doing the caring must do so for at least 35 hours a week and therefore be unavailable for work.

There are other conditions, too. While the carer can be married or single, he or she must be over 16 and under pensionable age, a UK resident and have lived here for at least 26 weeks in the past year. In addition, extra earnings are restricted, though "reasonable expenses" are permitted.

The DSS goes to great lengths to make sure this particular benefit is not abused and claimants already in receipt of other Social Security benefits are disbarred from it. The good news is that while you draw Invalid Care Allowance your National Insurance contributions are automatically credited to safeguard your future pension rights.

ATTENDANCE ALLOWANCE

The Attendance Allowance - which is not taxable and is usually paid with the State Pension - is meant for those disabled people who need attention and special supervision.

The rules allow for as wide a range of people as possible to draw it, but while there is no upper age limit, the person must have been resident in the UK and have been here for at least 26 weeks in the past year. In addition, they must have needed the "attention" of another person for at least six months.

That person might be a nurse or relative and does not have to live in. So the Allowance is even payable to those who live on their own and whose helpers visit.

There are two rates, a higher rate of £41.65 a week and a lower one of

£27.80 and the disability can be either physical or mental. Which rate you are entitled to will depend on how much attention your disability requires and how many of the ordinary functions you can perform for yourself. To get the lower rate you must fulfil either day-time or night-time conditions, for the higher Attendance Allowance you must fulfil both.

The day-time conditions require that the person claiming needs frequent attention to cope with normal bodily functions such as eating, going to the toilet or simply moving about. The Allowance is also available on the grounds that he or she needs supervision to avoid putting themselves or others in danger.

The night-time conditions are similar but "prolonged or repeated attention" must be needed during the night for periods of up to 30 minutes or at least twice. As a rough guide, those claiming the night-time allowance are generally more disabled. Someone who needs a carer to watch over them all through the night is also eligible.

As the Allowance is dependent on your medical condition it won't be paid instantly. And to qualify you must have been suffering the condition for six months, though you can put in a claim after three months and wait another three until it is actually paid.

What happens if someone claiming the Allowance has to go into hospital, where supervision is available round the clock? In this situation or if you have to go into a local authority home, for instance, the Allowance is stopped after four weeks.

If you are already in hospital or a council home, you can't claim the Allowance, of course, but should you be paying the full cost of private treatment or care then it will still be paid unless you are already getting Income Support towards these charges. If you travel abroad - for medical treatment perhaps - then you should still be able to get Attendance Allowance.

The Attendance Allowance is claimed through the local DSS office and it is a good idea when filling in the claim form to include a letter giving details of what you find particularly difficult to do and why. It's not just the physical things that will help you win the Allowance, but the side-effects like tiredness and lack of concentration, for instance.

You will have to undergo a medical examination - generally in your own home.

Not every applicant is successful the first time round. If this happens it is worth asking for a review of your case - statistics show that over half the review cases are eventually successful.

WIDOW'S BENEFIT

The Widow's payment is a single lump sum of £1,000 paid to those wives widowed under the age of 60. A widow over 60 will still get the payment, provided her husband was under the age of 65, had not retired or had an inadequate pension record when he died. This benefit is tax-free.

The actual Widow's Pension also depends on the husband's National Insurance contribution record which determines whether she gets the full amount of £52 a week or less. This is payable only to those widows who haven't yet retired, aged between 55 and 64 when their husband died. Once a widow is 60 she may be entitled to a State Retirement Pension in her own right based on her husband's record.

If a widow remarries then the pension stops - and the same applies if she lives with a man as his wife.

The Retirement Pension for Widows, which is also taxable, can be claimed by women who were over 60 when their husband died and is based on his contributions plus half any graduated pension. Again the maximum she can receive is £52, the same as the single person's retirement pension. In these circumstances, once she is retired no one is interested any longer whether she remarries or moves in with someone.

The claim for Widow's Pension starts as soon as a widow registers her husband's death with the Registrar. She will then be given a registration certificate and form to send to her local Social Security office who will give her the relevant claim form in return.

There is a special tax allowance, the Widow's Bereavement Allowance, which can be claimed for the first two years from the date of the husband's death.

MAKING AN APPEAL

Adjudication Officers decide on claims for Social Security benefits and anyone who disagrees with such a decision can complain to the Social Security Appeal Tribunal, which is a legally qualified body independent of the DSS.

The first step is to write to your local DSS office within three months of being turned down for something, including full details of your case. It's a good idea to enlist the help of your Citizens Advice Bureau.

Sometimes the decision may be reversed there and then under this review procedure. Otherwise it goes to tribunal.

Details of your case and a time and date for the hearing will be sent to you. Proceedings are always informal and you will receive travelling expenses. You are unlikely to be told the results then and there. The three panel members can only change the original decision if the regulations have been breached in some way, not just if the treatment seems a bit unfair; they cannot pay more money than the law allows.

MORE INFORMATION

If you want to know more about Social Security Benefits and National Insurance there is a freephone enquiry service - Freeline Social Security on 0800 666 555. This is for general advice on a host of different benefits.

NATIONAL INSURANCE BENEFITS - WHAT YOU GET

Benefit	Weekly rate 1990-91	Weekly rate 1991-92
Child benefit	7.25	8.25
One parent benefit	5.60	5.60
Pensions		
Single	46.90	52.00
Couple	75.10	83.25
Attendance allowance		
Higher rate	37.55	41.65
Lower rate	25.05	27.80
Sickness benefits		
Under pension age	35.70	37.60
Over pension age	45.00	49.90
Widow's allowance	£1,000 lump sum	
Mobility allowance	26.25	29.10
Unemployment, basic:		
Single	37.35	41.40
Couple	66.40	72.65

Chapter six

YOUR PERKS

Take advantage of all the concessions available

The good news is that there are a host of bargains waiting for you the minute you become an "official" pensioner. Some of them depend on where you live - some local authorities are far more generous than others.

But you will need some proof of your age. If you have a proper pension book this may be enough. Otherwise ask your DSS about getting an official ID card.

CHEAPER TRAVEL

British Rail has some particularly good offers - what's more some of them start before retirement. Anyone over 60, for instance, can apply for a Senior Citizen's Railcard entitling them to half-price, cheap day return fares. In addition you get a third off standard singles and returns, saver returns, some network breaks, 1st class single and return plus Rail Rovers.

For those still commuting to work, one of these cards can offer a better deal than some season tickets, certainly if you are not going in every day of the week and this is something well worth investigating. This is particularly true if you can travel off-peak. The current price for the Railcard is £16 a year.

If you are going by train to Europe some cross-Channel ferry companies will also grant a discount of up to a third when such voyages are part of a rail/sea journey. There are similar discounts available on some long distance British bus and coach routes, too. You may find some airlines also offer concessionary fares for pensioners.

Bus passes are available in some areas offering free travel, in others it's reduced, but in plenty of places you get nothing at all. This is a very important point when you think about moving. If you have to give up driving, as so many pensioners eventually do, it means relying on buses and paying the full fare will eat into your income.

As what's offered is usually down to individual local authorities, it does vary considerably. You may find that residents in the next street to you get free travel because it comes under a different authority to yours where there are, perhaps, no concessions at all.

But bus passes apart, as a rule it pays to check out just what reduction you can claim whenever you take a trip anywhere. Compare the costs and check out what's offered to pensioners. Going midweek, for instance, could sometimes halve what you have to pay.

There are reductions on certain holidays too, as well as some specially geared up for pensioners. You can get in virtually anywhere - from museums to art galleries - at a reduced rate or free of charge.

INSURANCE INCENTIVES

An increasing number of special insurance deals are coming on to the market for the over 50s, offering a variety of benefits like reduced premiums and extra services.

Motor insurance is one example - mature drivers are considered a "good risk", with statistics showing that young drivers are more likely to have accidents.

If you're a long-standing member of an existing car insurance scheme you'll have built up a good no-claims bonus and won't want to lose it by switching to another scheme. But insurance is a competitive business, and you may find you're able to switch to a scheme for the over 50s and take your no-claims bonus with you.

House insurance is another important area where your age could be of positive benefit. For although your age doesn't affect your chances of being burgled, statistics show that older people take more care of their homes and possessions and are more security-conscious. Insurers, recognising this, have a number of schemes that can reduce your annual premium.

Remember, too, that a number of insurance companies offer cheaper premiums if you can prove you belong to a Neighbourhood Watch scheme, if you have fitted good quality security locks and approved alarms.

Private medical insurance is another highly competitive area and there are important "perks" for the over 60s here - tax relief on premiums relating to the over 60s was introduced in April 1990.

Provided that the scheme a man or woman over 60 joins, or is already in, meets with the approval of the Inland Revenue, the person paying the premium gets 25% tax relief on the contributions. And a higher rate taxpayer is eligible for tax relief at 40% - the additional 15% is given via his tax code.

LOOKING GOOD

Virtually all hairdressing salons offer some "specials" for pensioners. Sometimes there's a special day when you can get a hairdo for about half price. The same applies to beauty salons - you may find manicures, facials and massage are all reduced for pensioners on a particular day.

Your local authority may run exercise classes with a reduced rate for pensioners - or even a special Keep Fit class specifically for them. Ask your Social Services Department at the Town Hall if they know about local concessions for pensioners. Many now keep a useful list which includes not just the things they run themselves, but some others from elsewhere.

Entertainment is one area where there are always concesssions. Most cinemas, for instance, will let you in cheap for certain performances as will theatres - though normally only for matinees.

BARGAINS GALORE

Many shops have discounts for pensioners . . . dry cleaners and shoe menders, for instance, may have special days when pensioners can get cut-price care.

If you want to know more about what shops in your area have on offer, it could pay you to contact your local Round Table or Chamber of Commerce. Your nearest library could help put you in touch.

Incidentally, if the libraries in your area still have a fines system for late books, this may well not apply to pensioners who can keep books out for as long as they like.

Of course, prescriptions are free for anyone over pension age - these days at £3.40 a time this can represent a big saving.

And at Christmas there is a special bonus paid to anyone receiving State Pension. You get this at the beginning of December every year. It should come automatically.

Chapter seven

TAX AND THE RETIRED

Your responsibilities explained

There's one thing you can be sure about - you may retire but the taxman never does! It's a sad fact that pensioners pay tax just like everyone else, yet there are still plenty of people about who believe that the moment they start to draw the State Pension they will stop paying tax.

This is quite untrue. Not only do you carry on paying Income Tax if your "income" is sufficient, but there may also be Capital Gains and Inheritance Tax to face as well.

The years on PAYE when having to fill in your tax returns was a rare event suddenly change with retirement. Your employer is no longer responsible for sorting out your tax - you are.

But it's not really that daunting. The secret is to understand how the system works . . . and to plan ahead. This should start with retirement itself.

If you are taking redundancy, for instance, and are one of the lucky few entitled to more than the maximum tax-free sum of £30,000 it would pay you to actually leave your company the other side of a new tax year.

This is because any allowances not used up on other parts of your income - and remember you are likely to be earning less when you retire - can then be used to cover for the money you get over the tax-free £30,000.

The opposite applies if all your pay-off comes into the tax-free category. Then it is at its most effective in a high-earning year.

THE GOOD NEWS

Big changes to the tax system which came into effect in April 1990 had a beneficial effect on pensioners and those coming up to retirement. For the first time married women were given some rights over their own money.

Up until April 1990 everything a wife earned was automatically added to her husband's earnings for tax purposes. It was always the husband's responsibility to fill in any tax forms - and, to add insult to injury, it was he who was entitled to all the tax rebates, including those due to her!

Independent Taxation changed all this - a husband and wife are now each responsible for their own tax. And most important, each are able to claim their individual tax-free allowances.

Under the old system, the Married Woman's Earned Income Allowance could be used only against the money the wife got from her job or pension plan. So any income she received from her savings would be tacked on to her husband's.

If he was in one of the higher tax brackets this meant her investment income was liable to his top rate of tax because, for tax purposes, it wasn't

regarded as her own money. And this was the case even if a couple opted for Separate Taxation. Then this only applied to earned income from a job or pension plan and a husband had to pay any tax due on his wife's investments.

Now wives have their own tax-free Personal Allowance which can be set against investment income if they choose.

The old Single Person's, Married Man's and Wife's Earned Income Allowance have all been phased out and under the new system everyone - male or female, married or single - has a Personal Allowance instead.

But the tax system still recognises marriage through the Married Couple's Allowance. This goes to the husband but, if he has insufficient income to use it in full himself, any surplus can be transferred to his wife for her to use up.

For the first time women over 65 qualify for age-related allowances in their own right.

In the age group 65-74 the Personal Allowance for the tax year 1991-92 is £4,020, for age 75 plus it's £4,180. But there is an income limit on this which was raised in the April Budget from £12,300 to £13,500.

What this means is that while a person's income stays under this amount then the Age Allowance is due in full.

Once it goes over the limit then it is progressively scaled down till it reaches the basic allowances.

It has been estimated that 3.75 million people will pay less tax as a result of Independent Taxation and the average reduction is expected to be about £250 a year.

Understanding 'income'

Not all the money you get is regarded as income as far as the Inland Revenue is concerned. But it's important to understand just what does come into this category . . . and what doesn't.

THIS IS INCOME

* Pensions including what you get from the State.

* Earnings from any kind of work you do, including fees you may charge for a part-time job.

* Investment income . . . the interest you get on savings where the tax hasn't already been paid for you. This applies if you have money in any unit trusts, for instance, or a bank deposit account.

* Profits from a business.

* All earnings from being self-employed.

* Social Security Benefits - Unemployment Benefit for example - and any payments under the Enterprise Allowance Scheme for setting up a business.

* Rents you get from letting out property or even a room in your house to help make ends meet.

* Any regular payments you get from elsewhere.

BUT THIS IS TAX-FREE

* Presents and gifts.

* Money you borrow.

* Money you inherit, because any tax owed will have already been paid.

* Winnings from gambling, unless this is your business.

* Premium bond prizes and pools wins.

* Money from certain investments.

* Some Social Security benefits - Attendance Allowance, Mobility

Allowance, for instance, and Income Support if it's paid for reasons other than unemployment.

* Special grants - for insulating your home, for example.

TAX TIMING

The tax year runs from April 6 to the following April 5 and any of the "income" described above that is assessed between these two dates is taxed at the basic 25% up to a ceiling of £23,700 after personal allowances and other allowable expenses have been deducted. Then tax is paid at the higher rate of 40%.

At the end of the book we give up to date tax tables and full details of the personal allowances for this tax year (1991-92). Every year these allowances and other personal reliefs are usually updated to take account of inflation or current Government policy.

But basically the following are the allowances you can claim:

THE PERSONAL ALLOWANCE: Everyone under the age of 65 has a tax free Personal Allowance regardless of sex or marital status. The special Age Allowance means this will be worth more for the over-65s and even more once you reach 75. A wife who doesn't work and therefore doesn't earn a salary can use her Allowance against any investment income she may have.

THE MARRIED COUPLE'S ALLOWANCE: On top of a personal allowance a married couple also get this extra allowance. Usually it will be set against the husband's income so that he will pay less tax. But if his income is low and he can't make use of all the allowance then the unused bit can be transferred to his wife.

SPECIAL ALLOWANCES: If you become eligible for the Age Allowance during a tax year you should get it automatically. But sometimes this can be overlooked. If you don't get it then contact your local tax office - address in the local phone book.

The normal Age Allowance for the over-65s can be backdated for up to six years, which could obviously give those eligible a handsome rebate. The higher Age Allowance was introduced in the 1987 Budget and those who have missed out on it can only claim back to that time.

There are other allowances that can be set against income. For instance, the Widow's Bereavement Allowance which is available from the date of bereavement until the end of that tax year - and for the following year provided she does not marry by the start of it.

There is also a Blind Person's Allowance which is available to registered blind people as individuals - in other words a blind couple can each claim it. In fact this particular allowance was doubled in the 1990 Budget to £1,080 less any tax-free disability payment received.

Of course, it's important to remember that these are allowances against tax - not grants - so there's no direct cash involved.

RELIEF V ALLOWANCES

On top of the tax allowances you can claim is the relief the Chancellor allows you on certain expenditure. The kind of expenditure included here is the interest you pay on the mortgage for your main home up to the £30,000 limit, special charity covenants, pension contributions and so on.

In addition, there is now relief on private medical insurance premiums for older people.

As a rule premiums on private medical insurance increase as you grow older, though there are now some special budget schemes designed for the over-65s.

Tax relief is available at the basic rate for certain approved schemes. And if the premium is being paid for you by a relative or friend then they can claim the tax relief . . . at the top rate, too.

If you still have a way to go before retirement you can sometimes also get additional tax relief through profit-related pay schemes at work.

To be able to claim relief for such a scheme means it has to be Government approved. There are certain conditions it has to meet before getting the official go-ahead. For example, a certain percentage of the workforce must be part of the scheme.

If it is just a matter of the senior management getting a share of the profits as a bonus, then the tax advantages do not apply.

OTHER TAX SAVERS

You get mortgage interest tax relief on your main home on the first £30,000 borrowed on the property. It isn't on offer for second, retirement or holiday homes and the 1988 Budget did away with the double relief on up to £60,000 that unmarried couples could claim when buying their own home. Now the relief limit applies only to the property rather than to the number of incomes coming into it.

If you are still working there are tax advantages to be had from contributions you make to occupational pension schemes, any additional voluntary contributions the scheme allows along with relief on contributions to the personal pension schemes favoured by the self-employed.

For approved schemes there is an earnings ceiling on which you can get this relief, as well as a maximum tax-free sum you can take when you retire.

With personal pension schemes those in the 51 to 55 age group can claim tax relief of up to 30% of their annual salary or 36% if aged 56 or over.

There is also an earnings cap for pension schemes.

As a result of the 1991 Budget anyone lucky enough to be earning more than £71,400 is not able to use money over this amount as a basis for contributions to an approved scheme or a personal pension plan. However, they can do so if they were already a member when the earnings cap was introduced in 1989.

As far as investments are concerned, tax at the basic rate is usually deducted at source from either interest or dividends. But people who fall into the higher rate band will have to budget to pay whatever extra is due from their net income at the end of the relevant tax year.

ALL ABOUT THRESHOLDS

Of course there are some people, particularly sections of the retired, whose "income" once they have claimed everything allowed is not high enough to make them liable to pay any tax at all.

Anyone in this situation should remember that once the basic rate tax has been deducted from any interest their savings have earned it cannot usually be reclaimed.

But as Composite Rate Tax was scrapped in April 1991 non taxpayers are now able to claim back any tax they have paid this way.

It's worth remembering that investments which pay "gross" - in other words before any tax has been deducted - can be a better bet.

If you are ever in any doubt about which of your investments have had the basic tax already deducted then ask. You should declare them anyway. You can't be taxed twice and the banks and other institutions will have told the Inland Revenue of any substantial pay-outs they have made to you.

But what if the Inland Revenue does make a mistake? You will get the money back . . . eventually.

The secret is to keep putting the pressure on until the money is returned.

However, you may have to wait till the next tax year.

Errors made in your favour are different. If you are charged too little tax and then the Inland Revenue discovers the error later you will get a demand for the outstanding amount.

If it's for a lot of money or you consider it unreasonable then you can use what's known as the Official Error procedure to get the matter fully investigated.

This won't always work in your favour but when it does, you will usually only have to pay part of the bill and, occasionally, none of it at all.

CAPITAL GAINS

If you have your own business, or lots of "assets" like a second home, shares or antiques then it won't just be Income Tax that interests you . . . there is also Capital Gains Tax to consider.

Very simply this tax is payable whenever you dispose of an asset. As far as the law is concerned "dispose" doesn't just mean selling something, but also includes giving it away, exchanging it for something else or even losing it - in a fire perhaps.

The tax you have to pay is calculated on what the item is currently worth even if you don't actually get any cash for it. But you only have to pay CGT on the increase in the value of the asset since a specific date - March 31, 1982 - and there is also a special allowance against inflation through Indexation Relief.

What this means is you only pay for the gain over and above inflation. In other words, some of your profit may still be tax-free.

TAX-FREE

There are some things you can sell and not have to pay any Capital Gains Tax.

Your home is probably your biggest asset but you don't have to pay CGT on any profit you make if you sell it as long as it is your only or your main residence.

If you have two homes then you can decide which one is your "principal private residence," to use official tax jargon.

You can sometimes be caught out if you sub-divide a large house into flats which you rent out or even if you simply use part of your home as an office and claim ordinary tax relief on it.

Any areas in your home deemed a business enterprise could then expose you to a capital gains penalty when you sell. In this situation you need to get professional accountancy advice - if you don't have an accountant then ask friends and family for personal recommendations.

SELLING UP

If you own a business or shares in a family company, then if you part with either you have to pay CGT. But if you are at least 55 when you take this step you could be eligible for something called Retirement Relief.

To qualify you must be selling up to retire and, provided you have been working there full-time as a director and have owned the business or shares for at least one year, you could escape CGT.

The relief increases for every year you have worked in the business up to a maximum of ten years.

You could be younger than 55 if you are retiring through ill-health. Otherwise it could be worth waiting till you reach this age before handing on your business so you qualify for this relief. If you don't you must expect to be taxed when you part with the business.

GIVEAWAYS

Every year you can dispose of things you own up to a "gains" total of £5,500 without having to pay CGT. Up until April 6 1990 this amount applied to single people and married couples had to share this tax saving between them.

Now that married couples are taxed independently they each have their own CGT tax-free sum. In other words as a married couple they'll be able to give away double . . . that's £11,000 gains for this tax year. A married couple don't have to pay any Capital Gains Tax on gifts to each other.

Before you reach the true taxable figure of any capital gain there are some other factors which are taken into consideration to bring that liability down. You can usually deduct the expenses involved in buying and selling the "asset," for instance.

WHAT YOU PAY

If you do dispose of a chargeable asset over and above your annual exemption limits it's taxed a bit like Income Tax. For individuals you'll be taxed at either 25% or 40%, depending on your income.

In other words, in a straightforward deal if the asset cost you £100 in 1982 and you sell it for £200 now you pay tax on the £100 profit . . . £25 at 25%.

"HEARING WELL HAS MADE LIFE WORTH LIVING AGAIN"

Marie Ford of Exmouth has been hard of hearing for years. Life became a misery as her hearing got worse. "Now thanks to my Scrivens mini-aid, I can hear really well again" she says "it's a wonderful invention".

Almost invisible

"I just pop it in when I wake up. It's so comfortable I don't know it's there. I don't think most people know I'm wearing it either. It's done a lot for my confidence and my happiness. It's been real value for money".

A big difference

"I've four grandchildren and spending time with them is my biggest joy. Time was when I couldn't hear what they were saying. Not anymore. Now I can join in family conversations and hear everything that is being said".

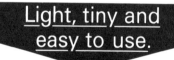

Light, tiny and easy to use.

If you are not deaf but simply hard of hearing, you can forget bulky, old-fashioned hearing aids. Thanks to modern science these tiny aids fit snugly in the ear so no-one need know you're wearing one.

SPECIAL OFFER

750 models to be given away absolutely FREE!

Post this special coupon before 22nd April and we will post you free, and without obligation, an actual size model (non-functioning) of this amazing tiny invention.

To Scrivens, FREEPOST, London NW5 1YB. (NO STAMP REQUIRED)

Please post me FREE and without obligation the gift for the hard of hearing plus special full-colour booklet. I am over 18.

Name _____ Address _____

Postcode _____ Telephone _____

Personal callers welcome at 245 Regent Street, London, W1. Tel: 071 734 4223   SR0401

67

Chapter eight

YOUR SAVINGS

Defending your family assets

In the past people relied on tins - one for the gas bill, another for groceries and the most neglected of all for any savings.

These days everything is far more sophisticated. For a start a series of tins like this is a huge temptation to passing burglars and, just as important, the money in them does not earn you any interest. And even if the inflation rate starts to go down your money will still be actually decreasing in value. Properly invested, it not only keeps pace with inflation but it can earn you a little something on top, too.

But where you should put it can be very confusing. As you hit retirement you will be bombarded with ideas for ways to invest your money, all billed as "foolproof" and often using jargon that most of us without a degree in economics cannot understand at all.

Only you can decide what's best and your decision will obviously have to be based on how much actual cash you have. If you have a fair bit you may decide to go for safety for most of it - and then use a little to do something more adventurous.

DEPOSITS AND INVESTMENTS

A deposit, according to the dictionary, is a sum placed in a bank, usually paying interest and not allowed to be withdrawn without notice. You put your money in and watch it grow . . . in a building society, bank or National Savings account.

Investments, on the other hand, are money put in stocks which can also be used for growth if you make the right choice. If you don't your money can actually start to diminish, but if you're lucky, it could do very nicely.

So how do you know what's best for you?

What you need is expert independent advice - and this can be one of the hardest things to find. The Citizens Advice Bureau is certainly a starting point - many areas now have money centres where you can get independent help and they will know about this. Alternatively try the IFA Promotion Ltd helpline on 081 200 3000 for the names of independent advisers in your area, or you can write to the Information Office, 33 St John's Street, London, EC1 4AA.

Think about the kind of investments that interest you most and then try and find a specialist in each field.

SAFETY FIRST

For most of us safety means building societies and banks. There is a lot of competition between the two for your savings. A growing number of

building societies are now offering high interest-paying accounts worth investigating. Your best bet is to work out how big an investment you can afford to make, whether you plan to save a regular sum each month and decide how long you can afford to lock your money away - and then shop around for the best deal.

You will find there's quite a difference in the accounts offered at various societies. Some pay most on large deposits and a minimum balance of, say, £10,000 for their top yielding account, while others will let you benefit like this for an initial stake of £250 and a promise to save a fiver a month.

The reason for this is pure competition. Nowadays, say some financial advisers, many of the real bargains are to be had with the smaller societies. Their overheads are lower - they may only have a few offices in the country instead of hundreds.

The banks have not been slow to respond to the competition from building societies. As a result many now offer a no charges deal for customers in credit, even paying interest on current accounts.

What all banks can offer, of course, are overdrafts which can obviously be useful. You can also get at your money quickly without losing out. But some people don't regard them as so good for money deposits as they are very much tied to the official bank rate and have far less room for manoeuvre than building societies.

Whatever you decide to do the secret is to make the best use of the services each offers and get them to work for you.

ALL ABOUT TESSA

Last year's Budget introduced a savings plan which makes saving with banks or building societies even more attractive. From January 1991 every adult is entitled to one Tax Exempt Special Savings Account (TESSA) free of tax provided the capital is left undisturbed for five years.

To cope with the investments of people who need income, interest can be withdrawn before the end of the five years but will be paid net of basic rate tax.

Investors will, however, receive the money which would have gone in tax (and interest earned on it) as a bonus at the end of that term.

The qualifying limits on TESSA are regarded as generous. Up to £9,000 may be deposited in a TESSA over five years - £3,000 in the first year and up to £1,800 after that. The maximum for regular savers is £150 a month.

But tax will have to be paid on the interest earned if any capital is withdrawn early.

It's been estimated that by using the scheme a basic-rate tax payer will find himself 11% better off at the end of the five years than if he had put

his money directly into a taxable account. For a person paying tax at 40% the figure rises to 18%.

Another important change for savers is the abolition of composite rate tax in April 1991. This means savers will be able to either get their interest on savings without paying any tax or to reclaim any that has been deducted.

Before 1991 building societies and banks paid interest after deduction of composite rate tax of 22% to all their savers. But those not paying income tax because they didn't work or earn enough could not claim this back from the Inland Revenue.

Under the new scheme only income tax payers will pay at the standard or higher rate.

NATIONAL SAVINGS

The days when you used to stick a 6d stamp on a National Savings card are long since gone.

Nowadays there are lots of schemes to choose from, often with the important advantage to many pensioners of paying interest without deduction of tax at source.

The precise conditions of who can hold what and of which account pays which rate vary. But the different National Savings accounts, bonds and certificates tend to rise and fall together.

The big advantage, of course, is that whichever plan you choose your capital is safe and if you do not pay income tax and are on a low income, then even lower than average interest rates can currently still represent a good deal.

Probably the most famous of the National Savings products are the index-linked certificates previously known as Granny Bonds, but now open to people of all ages, and Premium Bonds.

Index-linked certificates are linked to the retail prices index month by month with certain anniversary or terminal bonuses payable. But if you cash them in less than a year after the original purchase then you get your money back and nothing else.

Moving out of one issue into a more recent one can pay off depending how long you have held your bonds and what the interest advantage is.

Unfortunately there is no official source of advice on this, but the Post Office does keep lists of what your bond holding is currently worth and the lists are updated each month.

The table below shows the value of some Savings Certificates bought in recent years . . .

Issue	On sale	Value of £100 certificates after 5 years	Average annual return over 5 years
30th	13.2.85 to 9.9.85	£152.84	8.85%
31st	26.9.85 to 11.11.86	£145.92	7.85%
32nd	12.11.86 to 10.3.87	£152.12	8.75%
33rd	1.5.87 to 21.7.88	£140.26	7.00%
34th	22.7.88 to 16.6.90	£143.56	7.50%
35th	18.6.90 to 14.3.91	£157.42	9.50%

Reproduced by kind permission of the Director of Savings

There are lots of other things on offer for the saver, so it is worth keeping an eye on National Savings as they are announced.

At the time of going to press they were under review, hence we cannot give you the latest position.

UNIT TRUSTS

If you fancy investing in the Stock Market many financial experts see Unit Trusts as an excellent way for the newcomer to begin.

But it is only fair to point out that these were affected in the great Stock Exchange crash when millions of pounds were wiped off the value of Unit Trusts along with everything else. So you would still be taking a risk.

What the building society quotes you will actually get, whereas with a Unit Trust you could get a lot more. On the other hand you could get a lot less!

Unit Trusts or units are basically a basket of stocks and shares usually held in a particular field of investment or invested in a particular area of the world and managed by a specialist unit trust company.

They are set up under trust deeds approved by the Government.

As soon as the units are put together, they are offered for sale by the trust managers whose job it is to manage them successfully in order to produce a profit.

In addition they must promote the fund in order to attract more money to create additional units.

In effect this creates a large pool of money to buy shares while allowing the individual investor in the fund to come in and out of it easily.

Of course, the success or failure of a particular fund depends on the investment skill of the managers who actually choose the investments as well as managing the fund. Over the years they build up a considerable degree of knowledge in their specialist area.

There are now a number of different categories containing well over 1,000 different trusts.

At any one time the monthly league tables published in the financial pages of the national press will show the best and worst performers in particular sectors, together with the sector average.

But experts say you should not take too much notice of a fund's past performance - when you are buying what matters is the future performance and price. Get expert advice, though, if you are not sure.

Income is paid net of basic rate tax in the form of dividends, but this is one area where non-taxpayers can already reclaim tax paid. Higher rate taxpayers will have to pay more, of course.

The minimum investment varies from trust to trust and it is possible to spread an investment of, say, £1,000 across as many as 400 companies.

Again, experts think it is better when spreading the risk to select from more than one sector of Unit Trust.

That's because sometimes one sector hits a bad spot and under-performs for a long time. By having your money in different sectors this shouldn't cause you so many problems.

You usually buy direct from the unit trust houses or you can use the services of a professional adviser - try to find someone who is genuinely independent. If you work for a big company someone there may be able to advise on this, or ask friends and relations.

SHARES

One in four of us now have shares, often in the form of Unit Trusts as already described, or through a PEP. But a change in the 1990 Budget made them even more popular.

The present 0.5% stamp duty tax on share dealing is expected to be abolished towards the end of this year or early in 1992.

This and the fact that the Stock Exchange is to introduce a computerised dealing system is likely to reduce transaction costs and bring higher returns for small investors.

Lots of people start investing in shares at work.

Many large companies have schemes whereby employees save regularly in a save-as-you-earn scheme and then after a set period are allowed to use the money to buy shares in the firm.

But the fact is that unless you are very well off, most financial experts do not regard the eve of retirement as the time to start playing the stock market, with the exception perhaps of certain privatisation issues.

PEPS

Personal Equity Plans are a relatively new addition to the savings armoury. What these plans do is enable to you to build up your own "portfolio" of ordinary shares and trusts by saving a regular sum each month or using a lump sum to buy in.

There are now several hundred plans on offer from many different managers. Each one operates differently - sometimes the managers choose individual shares for you or you may pick your own. There will be a charge for setting this up and these vary, too.

There are restrictions on the amounts that can be invested this way - this year's Budget raised the figure from £6,000 to £9,000. You can do this by having two PEP plans whereas before you could only have one.

You can now put up to £6,000 in a general PEP and a further £3,000 in a corporate PEP.

In other words, you can buy a PEP on the open market with up to £6,000 and put £3,000 in a single company PEP, perhaps a company that you work for, or have worked for. This could be useful if you bought shares in your company through an employee share scheme.

The reason for the restrictions is the fact that profits from PEPs escape both capital gains and income tax. You don't even have to tell the Inland Revenue about them.

It's important to remember that this is an annual maximum - in other words if you put £6,000 into a PEP last year you can now invest £9,000 in two more and the dividends or profits you make on the total amount all escape tax.

Get independent financial advice before investing in a PEP.

GILTS

They may sound like something only for the very rich, but anyone with a bit of capital could consider investing in gilts.

What they are in fact are stocks issued by the Government as a way to fund spending, offering a fixed rate of interest and redeemable after a set time or on a specific date.

There are lots to choose from, each with their own individual characteristics, which makes for a complicated choice for the small investor. However, they are usually issued in blocks of £100 - though just to add to the confusion this is not what you actually pay but what you get back when you redeem them.

The rate of interest varies and the redemption dates do too - some have a date of less than five years away while others can run for 15 years or more.

Some Government stocks are linked to the cost of living. They work in the same way as the normal gilts but the nominal value and interest payments increase in line with inflation.

Which kind is best for you can sometimes depend on your tax situation, as income tax is payable on this interest.

You can buy gilts through the medium of a Unit Trust.

Alternatively you can use a stockbroker which will involve you in paying commission, or there's the National Savings Stock Register through the

Post Office. Dealing costs will be lower if you use the Post Office register, but transactions will take longer to go through.

For a £1,000 purchase the charge through the Register would be £4 which, says National Savings, compares well to a typical minimum charge for a stockbroker of £15.20.

You should be able to find a leaflet explaining all this at your local Post Office.

INSURANCE

Many experts see life assurance as being one of the most effective ways of saving over your working life. Such schemes have been running for many years and can be useful to someone who needs a regular income.

What these schemes do is tie up your money for a number of years and the capital investment is then used to buy you a temporary annuity - that's a special investment which gives you a proper income of a set amount at regular intervals.

Part of what you pay goes to an endowment assurance policy and this combination provides both for a net income and the capital repayment, provided the plan is maintained for the full term.

A more traditional alternative is to use, say, your retirement tax-free lump sum from your company pension to buy an annuity which will give you an income for the rest of your life.

What that income depends on, for the same sum invested, is your life expectancy - in other words your age when you start - your sex and the general interest rates.

The older you are the more generous the annuity will be, that's why many experts do not recommend them for anyone under 70.

One of the biggest drawbacks to these schemes can be inflation. When it's high then you can miss out as your income is eroded over the years - it is possible, for example, to lose well over half the payments' true value within 20 or 25 years.

INVESTMENT ADVISERS

There are many different savings and investment schemes on offer nowadays, and an even larger number of 'financial advisers' eager to help you choose the right one.

Its important, therefore, to choose the right adviser if you're to protect yourself from the rogues and incompetents that, sadly, still exist.

Many so-called advisers are simply salesmen concerned with only one company's products. That doesn't necessarily have to be a bad thing, but make sure that you ask any adviser you consult whether he is "tied" or totally independent.

The adviser to avoid at all costs is the one who lives only for today and is concerned more with the commission he'll earn on the insurance or investment policy he sells you than whether it is, in fact, the best one for your personal circumstances.

To safeguard yourself, make sure that any adviser you contact is a member of one of the "watchdog" bodies, known as Self Regulatory Organisations, set up under the Securities and Investments Board.

For more details of these watchdog organisations contact the SIB, whose address is given at the end of this book.

Anyone in the business of giving financial advice or selling investments must be a member of the relevant "watchdog" - but don't just accept the use of the SRO's logo on a business card as adequate proof.

'BEST' ADVICE

To do his job properly, a good adviser needs to ask questions about your financial situation, some of which you may find rather personal.

You don't have to answer all his questions, but it's in your interest to do so as the adviser is duty-bound to give you the "best advice" he can.

Once he has all the relevant information, the adviser will put together a suitable investment package for you. If he is a salesman "tied" to one company he will obviously have to try to do this from that company's products. But if there is nothing suitable for your requirements in that range, he must tell you so and not fob you off with the next best thing.

Once your requirements have been met, the company must send you a customer agreement setting out the services it is providing and the fee it is charging. Don't sign·on the dotted line unless you agree with this.

If you are subsequently unhappy with the way you have been treated by any member of a SIB "satellite" firm, then you can complain. Not covered under the complaints procedure, of course, are the usual risks of investment. But for the unfortunate saver who loses his money in an authorised firm that defaults or goes bust, there is some compensation available from a special fund known as the Investors' Compensation Scheme.

A debt of up to £30,000 can be claimed in full. And if you are owed more than this, you can also claim 90% of the next £20,000 . This means that the scheme is normally able to pay out up to £48,000 to each individual.

BUDGET PLANNER

ITEM	BEFORE RETIREMENT	AFTER RETIREMENT
INCOME BEFORE TAX:		
Employment		
Investments		
Pensions		
Any other source		
Total		
EXPENDITURE		
Taxes		
National Insurance		
Pension scheme contributions		
House insurance, inc contents		
Life insurance		
Others (not car)		
House:		
Community charge		
Water rates		
Rent or mortgage repayments		
Heat and light		
Repairs, decoration		
Household goods		
Furniture and carpets		
Transport:		
Fares		
Car tax		
Car insurance		
Car maintenance		
Petrol and oil		
AA/RAC subs		

ITEM	BEFORE RETIREMENT	AFTER RETIREMENT
Food and drink:		
At home		
Away from home		
Pet food and vet bills		
Entertainment:		
Papers, periodicals, books		
Sports and hobbies		
Theatre, cinema		
TV rental/licence		
Club subscriptions		
Classes & courses		
Holidays		
Personal spending:		
Hair and beauty		
Clothes, cleaning & repair		
Cigarettes and tobacco		
Confectionary		
Beverages		
Betting		
Charity		
Post and telephone		
Other		
Miscellaneous:		
Cards and presents		
Chemist		
Prescriptions		
Dentist		
Optician		
Other		
Other		
Total		

Chapter nine

MOVING ON OR STAYING PUT

Make the right decision on where to live

Giving up work often goes hand in hand with realising that retirement dream of moving to a little cottage in the country. Of course, this means leaving behind the home you have lived in for most of your working life, no doubt originally chosen for its proximity to the station or motorway rather than the roses growing over the door.

The only trouble is that your retirement choice of area is likely to be the same as that of many other pensioners. And this can produce a massive demand for social services which means a fall in standards . . . waiting lists for operations like hip replacements are always much longer in these areas, for instance.

Another problem is that the price of homes in these areas is often much higher than you expected, forced up by the competition. You could find that, far from helping you to raise some extra cash, selling up and moving to a popular retirement area actually leaves you out of pocket.

Alternatively, that tiny cottage with roses round the door may be at the top of a hill, in a remote village with few facilities, a very limited social life and no bus service.

The steep staircase which now forms part of its charm may well not seem quite so charming as you grow older. What suits you now may not seem so attractive when you reach 80 or 85.

CHECK IT ALL OUT

Trading down from a larger to a smaller property can still make good financial sense. But bear in mind that you may no longer have the advantage of a smaller rates bill, as the community charge is calculated in a different way.

So choosing whether to move or to stay where you are when you retire is a much more complex question than it appears at first. The type of house, its internal arrangements, the closeness and standard of social and medical services, the proximity of good shopping and what the public transport system is like all play an important part.

Remember, too, that the costs of moving may come to as much as a tenth of what you are paying for your new home and you could end up spending even more of your profit on decorating and furnishing.

Even if you are prepared for these costs you won't be able to keep on moving and facing them again, which is why whatever you decide to do on retirement requires such a lot of thought.

Just as important as the kind of place you decide to live in is how far away the chosen location is from your present address. It's easy to be dismissive about the part family, friends and even neighbours play in your life, but they are important and you will miss them all if you go too far away.

Of course you will make other friends, but if you have lived in one place for very many years it might not be quite as easy as you thought.

You should also make a list of all the other things that are important to you. If you are "townie" for instance, you will not only be used to public transport - even if you have a car now you may not always be able to use it - but also to having shops, libraries and other facilities within walking distance.

There could be a local theatre or cinema, for instance, which once you are retired you could make more use of . . . such things are unlikely to be found in country districts.

You will also be more used to noise and bustle than you realise - the peace of the countryside can sometimes seem almost sinister in contrast. Of course, each case is different, but before you come to any sort of final decision try to put yourself in the position of someone on their own, with no car and restricted mobility for whom outside interests are crucial.

WHEN THERE'S NO CHOICE

Of course not everyone is able to consider moving, particularly those in rented accommodation. And even if you own your own home, the prospect of a smaller income may make staying put difficult, if not impossible.

These days lots of us are what the economists call asset-rich, cash-poor. Our basic cash pension will just about cover our everyday needs, while our homes have appreciated to a handsome five-figure sum we can't get our hands on.

But it is possible to realise a large part of the value of our present homes and there are some simple ways to use it to raise money.

One of the easiest is to let part of it out. Provided you continue to live there you will not run into any capital gains tax problems. Renting provides a useful source of income and, for those living on their own, some welcome company too.

You would have to declare any rental income for income tax, of course, and this could affect any Social Security benefits you are claiming.

Against this you should be able to write off about 10% of the rental against income tax for things like repairs.

If you do decide to take this step make sure any lodger you accept has been thoroughly vetted - go by personal recommendation only.

Let for no more than six months to start with, in case you change your mind and, most important, see that you understand all the legal implications and the terminology involved. Your Citizens Advice Bureau should be able to help here.

For a few, one stage up from taking in lodgers is to rent out part of their home as a separate flat, either by converting it or by making use of one which is already there.

You become the "granny" as it were and take over the granny flat. It does not particularly matter whether the accommodation is furnished or unfurnished since, under the latest Housing Act, you should be able to repossess the property either way - though you must get proper advice on this.

Your lodger becomes a tenant with certain rights whilst you are a landlord with certain responsibilities. You can, for instance, be forced by the local authority to carry out essential but expensive repairs.

UNLOCKING THE CASH

There are other ways of raising money on your own home while still living there. Home Plans are specifically designed as a way of unlocking useful capital while allowing you to stay put. Of course, there is a price to pay - the two main types of plan on offer will make a big hole in your "estate" .

But both are worth investigating as a growing number of retired people living in expensive homes are struggling to make ends meet, and this is one way of making the most of what they own.

However, if you do decide to take things further, make sure you consult a solicitor. If you haven't already got one then ask friends for personal recommendations or contact your Citizens Advice Bureau - the address is in the phone book.

THE HOME INCOME PLAN is currently the most popular scheme and is also sometimes known as a Mortgage Annuity.

Basically this means that a loan (or mortgage) is given to you against your home and the money is used to buy an annuity - a special investment which gives you a yearly income of a set amount, in this instance guaranteed for life.

As well as the money that comes regularly to you, another part of the income from the annuity goes to pay off the interest on the loan.

In other words, this is rather like a second mortgage. Because your home is still yours it is you who benefits should house prices start to rise again, as predicted by some experts.

And one of the main attractions of the Home Income Plan is the fixed rate of interest which has stayed at 8.25% since 1980.

The original loan does not have to be repaid during your lifetime but is repayable on death - or, with a couple, on the death of the survivor. The minimum age to qualify for a plan is 69, but if you are a couple then your combined ages must total 145.

How much money you can raise for the company to buy your annuity is generally limited - somewhere between £15,000 and £30,000.

However, if property prices do start to take off again the scheme offers facilities to increase the income you get.

But you never get a loan invested on your behalf that's worth the full value of your home - it's usually around a maximum of three quarters of what it's worth.

Though most plans refer to houses, you can be eligible if you live in a flat or maisonette provided you have a long enough lease. It is only if you have tenants or some other outstanding loan that you may be turned down.

As the plans are all about risk, the odds are you will be offered more income the older you are.

Sometimes you may also be able to get an immediate cash sum. This will mean less money every month and most experts recommend caution over this.

And what if a policy holder died early, well before he or she had benefited from the annuity but still with the loan left to repay?

Plan organisers have thought of this and often offer special capital protection option policies which, while reducing the income a little, do at least ensure that an "estate" needs to repay only a proportion of the sum borrowed in such situations.

Nevertheless, because some part of the loan is repayable on death it means what's available to be passed on to the family is obviously reduced.

As far as tax is concerned, basic rate tax payers will receive the income after tax has been deducted at source.

Such plans will not affect the tax you pay on your present income, so this is good news for those in higher tax bands. If you don't pay any tax at the moment you can often get the income without the tax deduction, which obviously improves the benefit, so check this out carefully.

HOME REVERSION SCHEMES are different because you actually sell all or part of your home in return for a cash sum plus the lifetime right to continue living there.

But the valuation of your property on which the cash sum is based will appear to bear little relationship to the current market value, even in its present low state.

A £100,000 home, for instance, will only raise about £50,000 as a home reversion. The money you get would depend on your age. For instance, a woman of about 66 would receive around 34% of the value whereas a woman of 85 would get about 60%.

The valuation is based on how long the company calculates you will stay there as a sitting tenant paying them nothing in return.

Some schemes are much better than others and build in safeguards that enable you to benefit from any future increase in the property's value, even if you no longer own it through some sort of profit-sharing scheme.

It goes without saying that it is more important than ever to get proper legal advice on schemes like this. For example, it is crucial to check the terms of the lease regarding your security of tenure.

While you get a bigger cash sum from these schemes than you do with the home income plans, you are giving away a lot more in return. And the money can be invested to provide you with an annuity income if you prefer. If you take a capital sum your tax position would depend on where you invest the money.

QUESTIONS YOU SHOULD ASK

As with anything involving money and where you live, there are all sorts of hidden dangers with these schemes. There are others not featured here where the loan actually increases as the years go by. Instead of giving the home owners cash for the rest of their lives they actually end up owing a lot of money.

That's why before you consider using your home as a way to raise some income you must get independent financial advice. If you don't know how to find this then go to your Citizens Advice Bureau or Legal Advice Centre - you'll find the address in your phone book or from your local library. Or contact IFA Promotion Ltd - address and phone number at the back of the book - for the names of local independent financial advisers in your area. You could also contact Age Concern at 1268 London Road, London SW16 4EJ. Tel: 081 679 8000.

You must also use the solicitor of your choice, not one acting on behalf of the people selling you the plan. And before you do anything check out the following questions:

• What happens if you want to move? This is possible with a Home Income Plan.

• Are you receiving any kind of State Benefits that would be affected by an improvement in your financial situation? If you lose them as a result will the money you get from the plan make up for this?
• Do you know all the costs involved? Administrative fees, legal costs, insurance and, most important, of all who is responsible for them? Are any refundable later?
• Have you sorted out the tax situation? Not all the schemes work to your advantage on this.

PAYING THE BILLS

Whether you decide to move or to stay put you will still have to meet the bills for repairs and improvements plus heating out of a reduced income. That's why it can pay to investigate the grants that are available for major structural work, plus insulation, that in turn will reduce your heating costs. The rules and conditions under which improvement grants are made vary, depending on where you live as much as on the work to be done. Most are given at the discretion of the local authority. People on Income Support or Housing Benefit in areas where there is a special Insulation Project may get extra help.

RETIREMENT HOMES

Special retirement homes are big business now. In the past sheltered housing, as it was called, was provided by local authorities, charities and housing associations and nearly always involved long waiting lists. But these days easy-to-manage, purpose-built and self-contained units are on offer in the private sector.

The aim of these places is to give as much independence for as long as possible in a safer and more secure environment, avoiding the institutional feel of the traditional old people's home. The help on offer is discreet - someone to turn to in an emergency as well as a good security system.

If you do decide to consider such a place, when you visit look out for the tell-tale signs of a hastily conceived development . . . the steps where there should be ramps, the lack of hand rails, badly sited lighting or high kerbs.

None of these things may be a problem to you but they say a lot about the amount of thought that has gone into the development.

Retirement homes are certainly not cheap. There is usually a lower age limit of, say, 55 for prospective buyers and any money left over from the sale of your former home may have to be put aside to cover service charges which, not surprisingly, tend to be high.

RETIRING ABROAD

Selling up and taking the first plane out to somewhere exotic is a retirement dream many of us share. It can work . . . but only if you do your planning carefully.

You need to know not only if you can draw your pension in the country of your choice, but also who will look after you as you grow older, what happens if you become ill and how you will make yourself understood.

The basic State Pension may not seem much but it is linked to the cost of living and often forms a major part of a pensioner's income.

The fact is there is no difficulty getting it paid anywhere in the world provided you notify the Department of Social Security's special overseas branch in Newcastle in advance of emigrating. They can then arrange for it to be paid to you in the location of your choice in much the same way as through a Giro here.

However, there are problems in some countries - Canada for instance - where your pension is paid but only at the rate applying when you left the UK.

In other words, if you leave this year and are getting the current £83.25 a week pension for a couple, that is what you will still be getting in 10 years. So it is effectively frozen from that time on, with no cost of living or further increases.

The good news is you can get these increases in countries where the UK has a reciprocal agreement - this includes all our Common Market partners and the most popular retirement place of the British, Spain. The list also includes Bermuda, the Channel Islands, Switzerland and the USA.

Company pensions have no restrictions on where they can be paid either, but should the two when added together put you into a basic tax bracket, there are certain steps you will have to take in order to satisfy the Inland Revenue as to your overseas status.

You will need to get expert advice on this, but a lot depends on whether you plan to return home from time to time - and most important, whether you keep a place in the UK in which to stay.

Once you do this you will be deemed resident here for any year in which you return, however short your stay, and whether or not you own the accommodation. Your best bet once you start thinking about emigrating is to get help . . . the Citizens Advice Bureau should be able to suggest a suitable expert or you may find your bank helpful here. Both the Inland Revenue and the DSS have leaflets about retiring abroad.

THEM AND US

If you think our tax system is complicated, just wait till you see what faces you in some of the countries where you may be considering retiring! Who would know, for instance, that French death duties vary conversely with the proximity to the family?

The closer the relatives are the less they have to pay, starting with the spouse. Second cousins twice removed are treated very differently from sons and daughters.

Portuguese rates, on the other hand, are two-tiered with one part payable on the land at 14% of its value and the other on the rent from or the assessed rentable value of the property at 18% .

All this makes doing your home work about life in the country of your choice so important. Start in the UK with the embassy information service and the commercial attache. It is the latter who will have more day-to-day British contacts, will generally speak better English and will certainly be the best informed about the tax and legal situation in his or her own country.

Chapter ten

SORTING OUT YOUR AFFAIRS

Your inheritance checklist

Only one in four of us ever get around to making a will . . . and one reason is that lots of us genuinely believe we haven't anything to leave.

But the fact is we all have something . . . anyone who owns a house, for a start, probably has a very considerable amount. But even if you aren't a property owner you might have a gold watch, your own car or even some money in the bank.

Others assume a will isn't necessary because his or her partner will automatically inherit the lot. But this doesn't always happen - sometimes a couple die together, for instance - and in any case it will still involve those who are left in a lot of complicated work during their time of mourning.

What a will does is make it clear exactly what is to happen to your "estate" - the legal term for the value of all your assets once any tax, debts and funeral expenses have been paid.

In addition a will appoints the people you choose to sort everything out for you, as well as making any special requests for sums of money to go to, say, a pet cause once all your immediate family has been taken care of.

GETTING ADVICE

Most stationers and even some post offices have special forms you can fill out at home when you come to make your will, but even so it's still very easy to make mistakes.

For instance, two witnesses are required by law when you actually sign your will and they must be there together - if one went to answer the door then, strictly speaking, the will would no longer be valid.

What's more neither of the witnesses must be beneficiaries in any way or they would not be allowed to receive whatever you had left them. And this applies to the husband or wife of those witnesses, because he or she benefits indirectly.

There are other potential pitfalls too. Even though the witnesses do not need to know what the will contains, for instance, a blind person is disbarred. And should you have second thoughts and want to amend the will on the spot, all three of you would have to sign the amendments.

Lots of people also go wrong in the way they phrase their bequests - they get the name of the charity slightly wrong or they leave their "favourite" necklace to someone without describing it in more detail and then no-one can remember which one it was.

Pet names for members of the family can also cause problems - one man left everything to "mummy", but he called his wife by this name as well as his mother who was still alive at the time.

It doesn't cost the earth to get to heaven . . .

In fact making a will can cost you only a modest amount.

Your bequest will help Barnardo's carry on its pioneering work with nearly 20,000 children, young people and their families.

More than half the funds we need come from bequests just like yours.

Please help us through your will.

For more information please return the coupon.

Barnardos

Barnardo's - a registered charity No. 216250

Another potential problem is that the law of inheritance and wills is different in Scotland from that in England and Wales. But many of the special will forms designed for English law are sold in Scotland, which can give rise to problems.

The way in which wills need to be signed in Scotland is also different - if the will is in your own handwriting, for example, witnesses may not be necessary.

WHAT YOU PAY

The simplest way to cut out all this potential hassle is to consult a solicitor. It won't cost you that much and it is a one-off payment. Costs vary depending where you live, but you shouldn't have to pay much more than £40 plus VAT outside London.

And you probably won't have to pay anything at all, or certainly only a much reduced fee, if you appoint one of the solicitors at the firm to act as an executor.

A solicitor appointed as an executor will have to be paid for his professional services after your death, though in Scotland it is rare for a solicitor to make any specific charge in relation to his duties as an executor - his charges will relate to the administration connected with the legal work instead.

There are provisions for those on low incomes to be entitled to legal aid and the CAB can explain just who is eligible.

If you are not quite sure about the duties of executors, these are basically the people you appoint to be in charge of your affairs and to see that your wishes are actually carried out.

They start to deal with your affairs from the moment of death. There can be a great deal of work involved, so it is tactful to ask the people you choose, if they're not your solicitor, if they mind before actually naming them in your will.

If you are married and both of you plan to leave virtually everything to each other then you could become each other's sole executor, provided your affairs are straightforward.

The only trouble is that the bereavement itself could make this a particularly upsetting and difficult job.

That's why a better idea can be to also appoint one, competent close friend each to help the survivor sort everything out sympathetically.

Most "estates" are far from complicated but it does help to keep all the relevant papers in one place known to all the family.

PLANNING YOUR WILL

Even if you use a solicitor you still need to work out what you want to happen to your "estate". And there are other things to think about, too.

If you own your home jointly with your spouse or partner under what's legally defined as a "joint tenancy", remember that your co-owner will automatically inherit your share, whatever you say in your will.

If, however, you have a "tenancy in common", then you have the right to leave your share to whoever you want. These terms should have been explained to you by the solicitor when the title deeds were drawn up.

The deeds are held by the building society or bank from where you borrowed the money for your mortgage and you can check the terms there if you aren't sure.

Sole owners of a property can obviously leave it as they choose. Couples in rented accommodation need to check with their landlord or a solicitor what happens if one of them dies.

The surviving partner can almost invariably have the tenancy transferred if they want - but now is the time to make sure.

ALL IN THE FAMILY

You also need to think about how you would like your children to benefit. If they are still young they can't actually inherit until the age of 18.

You can specify an even later age if you fear they wouldn't be responsible enough then . . . lots of people use 21 or even 25 instead.

In Scotland the law on wills is very different, and it should be noted that, even if you leave a will, the law provides that certain relatives may be entitled to claim against your estate contrary to your will. This is not the same as them actually contesting your will.

Accordingly, in Scotland unless your spouse and your children, and the children of any child of yours who has died, is prepared to agree to the provisions in the will relating to them, you are not able to do as you would like.

Nearly all pension plans allow for payments to the surviving widow or widower once the actual recipient dies.

If you aren't married but have a long-term partner you can nominate him or her as a beneficiary. Contact the trustees of the personal pension scheme you belong to - the address should be on the policy document.

You can also leave what's legally known as a "specific bequest" to individual friends or an organisation . . . for example, a favourite piece of jewellery. If it's a specific sum of money you want to leave then it's known as a "pecuniary bequest".

Both the gift and the chosen recipient should be clearly identified - be sure you have a proper description of the item along with the full address of the person named.

If you have a favourite charity you want to support, it won't just have a name but also a registration number. It pays to use both - your local reference library should have a book containing these or you could contact the charity direct and ask for its details.

THINGS TO THINK ABOUT

In a will you can say whether you want to be cremated or buried as well as giving details of the way you would like your funeral conducted. You can name a particular church for the service, for example, along with the hymns you would like to have sung or the music you want played.

It's also customary to leave a token bequest to a non-professional executor. If you are worried about the cost of the funeral itself and the worry this might cause your partner, you could consider taking out a funeral payment plan to cover the cost.

In a survey sponsored by Age Concern last year, the range of plans offered by a company called Chosen Heritage were deemed to offer good value for money. But a reminder from that firm - if you do take out such a plan, make sure your family know you have done so and with which company.

Once all your wishes have been carried out and all expenses have been deducted what's left is called your residuary estate. The last thing you have to decide is who you want to receive or share in this.

Then once your will has been drawn up for you by a solicitor you must decide where it should be kept.

It's a good idea to keep a copy of it with all your documents, like birth and wedding certificates, for instance. With it there should be a note saying where the top copy is - probably safest with the solicitor who drew up the will for you in the first place, or your bank.

CHANGING YOUR WILL

You can change your will as often as you like . . . the valid one is the last one you ever make.

For single changes like an extra bequest or an update on the money you wish to leave, all that's needed is something called a codicil which is the legal term for an amendment. However, because it is a legal document it must be signed and properly witnessed.

FORGET ABOUT FUNERAL COSTS!

- Chosen Heritage provides a guaranteed funeral when required, at *today's* price, at any point in the future.

- Chosen Heritage spares trouble and expense for your family.

- Chosen Heritage gives you peace of mind, knowing that all the arrangements are made and paid for.

Thousands of people have joined the Chosen Heritage scheme so they can forget about funeral costs. These are not insurance policies but a practical way to make arrangements in advance.

Simply return this coupon for your free brochure or call now on **FREEPHONE 0800 525 555**.

Completely confidential. No salesman will call.

RECOMMENDED BY

AGE *Concern*

CHOSEN HERITAGE LIMITED FREEPOST, EAST GRINSTEAD, RH19 1ZA

CUSTODIAN TRUSTEE: BARCLAYS BANK PLC

selected 'Best Buy' in recent survey

Please send me your brochure, with no obligation.

Name: _____

Address: _____

_____

_____ Post Code: _____

When more substantial changes are involved it's probably easier to draw up a new will altogether, but again it makes sense to seek legal advice.

A will is automatically cancelled - or revoked to use the correct legal term - on marriage in England and Wales, unless it was drawn up specifically with this in mind.

This does not, however, apply in Scotland.

With a divorce after a will has been made, then legally it will be interpreted as if your ex-spouse had died on the day your marriage was officially ended. Any gift left to him or her will go to the person who gets the residuary estate.

Again, the position is different in Scotland.

WHAT HAPPENS WHEN THERE'S NO WILL?

If someone dies "intestate" or without making a will then, in England and Wales, where everything he or she owns actually goes depends on personal circumstances. For instance, if the person was married with children, then the surviving spouse gets the "chattels" or belongings, plus a lump sum up to £75,000. Anything left over would be divided equally in two - one half invested for the surviving spouse, who will get the interest but not the capital which passes to the children, including illegitimate ones, on his or her death. The other part is given to any adult children or invested on their behalf if they are under 18.

If the deceased person wasn't married or had no children there are laws governing exactly where the "estate" should go.

But by not making a will the family left faces a lot of sorting out. There can be other problems, too. For instance, if the couple have a tenancy in common as opposed to a joint tenancy and one of them dies intestate, the surviving spouse could end up losing their home because it becomes part of the estate to be divided automatically between family members.

A CHALLENGE

Close members of your family or other dependants - like someone you live with and support - may be able to challenge your will if you have made no specific provision for them. So if you have strong reasons for feeling that a close family member should not be entitled to anything then an explanatory letter to this effect should be placed with the will.

In Scotland, as has already been explained, close members of the family have specific claims irrespective of whether or not a will has been made. Challenging a will is, accordingly, uncommon in Scotland.

CHECKLIST

It helps to make a list of what you want to happen before you see a solicitor to draw up your will.

Put down as many details as you can - many solicitors base their charges on time and anything that cuts this down should help you. In particular, be sure to include:

* Executors' names and addresses

* Assets:
Your house and whether it's owned jointly, rented and so on
Mortgage details
Investments and insurance details
Pension
Other valuables - car, jewellery, antiques and so on
Bank and building society accounts and their numbers
Other savings

* Any debts

* Beneficiaries (those you want to inherit)
Specific bequests
Any pecuniary bequests
Charitable gifts - and check the name and registration number of the charity if you can

* Special wishes

* Copies of the will - where do you want them to go?

DEATH DUTIES

Time was when death duties were something you read about in the papers. Only the very rich were involved.

Nowadays it's possible that anyone with a house worth more than £140,000 could be affected. This is the point at which Inheritance Tax can bite into your "estate" at a rate of 40%, meaning your savings and your home. That's why it pays to understand how this tax works and what you can do to ease the burden for your family.

Inheritance Tax used to be known as Capital Transfer Tax, though of course most of us still think of it as death duties. But the fact is it isn't just a tax paid on inheritance when someone dies. IHT may also have to be paid on gifts made during your lifetime.

There's only one rate of IHT for the 1991-92 tax year - 40%. But any tax you have to pay on what are lifetime gifts is paid at half this rate - 20% .

It's a complicated subject but, as a very rough guide, what you need to do is work out how much your "estate" is likely to be - this basically requires you to add up everything you own - property, cash, savings and investments.

If it looks likely to be under £140,000 you won't have to pay IHT. Once you go over you should start taking some action.

TAX-FREE GIFTS

To trim your "estate" there are tax-free gifts you can make as well as allowances you can use each year.

As a very rough guide, whatever you give away to your husband or wife is tax-free, whether it's your old car or a luxurious mansion in the country!

Every year you can also give away tax free:

* Gifts up to £250 each to any number of individuals

* To someone else you can give up to £3,000.

* Money gifts regarded by the taxman as "normal everyday expenditure" . Into this category could come pocket money for your grandchildren or cash sums you use as a way to thank someone in the family - for helping out with the garden, for example.

* Special occasion gifts are also allowed - you can give an extra £5,000 to your children when they marry and £2,500 when it's each of your grandchildren's turn.

*Anyone else you know who is getting married can have a gift of up to £1,000 tax-free

If you have lots of money or property to spare over the IHT limit of £140,000 it could be worth investigating something called Potentially Exempt Transfers, or PETs, as they are called.

What you do here is put off paying any tax on a special gift until you die - but if you live for at least another seven years after making the gift then you won't have to pay any tax at all.

This can be one way of giving your home to your children. But it isn't that straightforward - there are all sorts of conditions which need going through with an expert.

If you don't know where to go then, again, your Citizens Advice Bureau is a good place to start.

Chapter eleven

ALL IN
A GOOD CAUSE

Helping others in
your spare time

If there's one good thing about retirement, it's that it brings with it all the extra free time you want to do the things that you never had time for in the past.

It's a point well illustrated by the huge numbers of people who get involved with charity work once they've finished full-time employment.

Most of us have a pet cause and at last, in retirement, we can actually devote a lot of time to it.

Voluntary work is one of the most popular areas that people in retirement choose to devote their time to. It's a fact that, today, most charities in Britain are staffed by volunteers . . . in fact, charity is run by charity.

And these days it's not just flag days and sponsored walks that need organising - fund raising is much more sophisticated and varied, requiring skills that many retired people have to offer.

If you were in management, for instance, you will have all kinds of useful executive experience to offer.

People with personnel experience will be able to help in a charity's more public work. Those with secretarial skills will find that there's always a need for 'backroom' help with the mountains of paperwork that a charity both attracts and generates. And manual workers will find there's no shortage of demand for their practical skills.

Whatever job you did during your working life, there will be something you can enjoy doing in retirement - and you'll have the added satisfaction of knowing that you are really helping a cause you care about at the same time.

It may be that the charity you choose to help is one that you've been helped by, or come into contact with, in the past.

Many of the volunteers who work for the hundreds of medical charities, for instance, have first-hand experience of dealing with the consequences of specific illnesses, while widows form the bulk of those who work for bereavement support groups.

It might be a political party you care about, a specific campaign in your area against a new supermarket, perhaps, or a road that will ruin a particular village or treasured view of the countryside.

Whatever your reasons, your help and vast experience of life will be valued. Charity work is, indeed, one of the most obvious examples of an activity where your age could be used to positive advantage, rather than being held against you.

What's more this sort of work is a great way to make new friends and replace some of those you had at work - an important consideration.

You'll have the opportunity to mix with people from all different age, social and ethnic groups and will, undoubtedly, find the work both absorbing and stimulating. It will probably teach you a thing or two, as well!

GETTING STARTED

The first step if you want to get involved in some charity work is to make a list of exactly what you have to offer. Your skills, your experience, even your hobbies and practical things as well - like being able to drive or cook.

Next work out just how much time you can afford to give - days or hours each week or so much time in a month.

Then find a charity or campaign with which to get involved.

You could write to the head office of your particular favourite - if you don't have the address, ask at the library.

In the letter list the kind of skills you have to offer and the time you can spare. It's best to be honest about this from the start, so no-one enters into the arrangement on false pretences..

Or look in the local paper to see if there are details about planned charity activities in your area or appeals for help.

OTHER WAYS TO HELP

If you decide you haven't as much time to help as you thought, you could make a covenant to your favourite charity instead.

A Deed of Covenant is a legal document used for pledging a certain amount of money regularly to a charity of your choice. You have to commit yourself to pay a fixed amount of money every year - or more often, if you prefer - for a period of more than three years. After three years the money given qualifies for income tax relief.

But some donors miss out on this because the Deed has not been properly drawn up - it has to comply with the requirements of general non-tax law.

All that is necessary is to complete a legally-effective, simple form and get your signature witnessed by one other person.

The Inland Revenue has designed two simple 'model' forms as guidance - one for England and Wales and the other for Scotland. You will find them at the end of the chapter. If you follow the wording of these forms when drawing up a covenant then you'll know it will be acceptable to the Inland Revenue. The 'model' deeds are drawn up in 'net' form, which means that you enter on the form the amount of money you actually pay, rather than the gross amount.

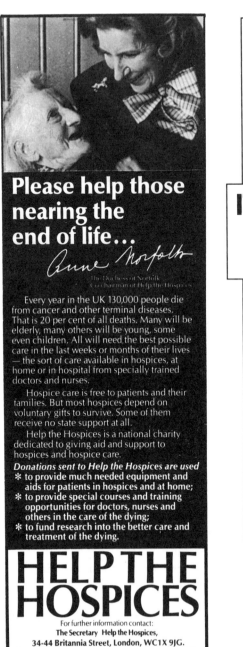

Please help those nearing the end of life...

Anne Norfolk

The Duchess of Norfolk
Co-chairman of Help the Hospices

Every year in the UK 130,000 people die from cancer and other terminal diseases. That is 20 per cent of all deaths. Many will be elderly, many others will be young, some even children. All will need the best possible care in the last weeks or months of their lives — the sort of care available in hospices, at home or in hospital from specially trained doctors and nurses.

Hospice care is free to patients and their families. But most hospices depend on voluntary gifts to survive. Some of them receive no state support at all.

Help the Hospices is a national charity dedicated to giving aid and support to hospices and hospice care.

Donations sent to Help the Hospices are used
* **to provide much needed equipment and aids for patients in hospices and at home;**
* **to provide special courses and training opportunities for doctors, nurses and others in the care of the dying;**
* **to fund research into the better care and treatment of the dying.**

HELP THE HOSPICES

For further information contact:
The Secretary Help the Hospices,
34-44 Britannia Street, London, WC1X 9JG.
Facsimile: 071 278 1021 Telephone: 071 278 5668
A REGISTERED CHARITY No 289 345

IT'S MIGHTIER THAN THE SWORD.

A signature on a will.

It can go a long way to provide for the ex-servicemen and women of Erskine Hospital.

We need to raise more than £1 million worth of public donations every year.

We need to maintain expert medical care.

We need to provide the special facilities that our many disabled residents require.

That's why it's so important that people remember us when they make a will.

Donations or bequests should be made payable to the Princess Louise Scottish Hospital (Erskine Hospital), Bishopton, Renfrewshire. (Correspondence to the Treasurer, I. W. Grimmond, B.Acc, C.A., at the hospital. Telephone: 041-812 1100.)

If the gift you make to the charity comes out of your taxed income - in other words you have already paid tax on it - then the charity can claim back the tax paid from the Inland Revenue.

So if you are paying tax at the basic rate of 25%, for every 75p you pay the charity, it can claim back an extra 25p.

You are not normally allowed to receive any benefit in return for your covenant, but some charities do give membership benefits in return for covenanted payments. In the case of ordinary small subscriptions, the benefits available to subscribers are, in practice, ignored by the Inland Revenue if they are worth less than 25% of the subscription.

And if the charity's sole or main purpose is to preserve the national heritage or wildlife, the benefit of a member's right of entry to view the charity's property is left out of the account altogether.

An important consequence of the introduction of Separate Taxation last year is that a husband and wife are now treated separately when they covenant.

TAX-FREE

Money given to charity in any form during your lifetime or under your will is always tax-free.

You don't have to pay Inheritance Tax either on payments made for what are deemed "national purposes".

This covers gifts to a favourite museum perhaps or even to a political party, as long as it is one of the main parties. To be classed a main party it must have two MPs in the House of Commons - or one MP plus 150,000 votes at the last election.

If you want to leave money to a pet cause or charity in your will then you could contact its headquarters for details of the kind of legacy you can give.

Again the library should have the address - and most important, where charities are concerned, make sure you get the charity's official number to include in your will so there will be no problems in identifying the charity you mean.

Under the new Gift Aid scheme which came into effect in October 1990 there is another way to give cash to a favourite charity and, depending how well off you are, escape some tax at the same time.

The scheme will allow charities to claim back the basic rate tax - currently still 25% - on donations between £600 and £5 million. And donors in the higher tax bracket, paying at 40%, will then be entitled to claim 15% tax relief on the gift.

So how will this work? The donor gives the charity £750 which is the equivalent of £1,000 before basic rate tax. The charity - which must be a recognised one - then gets an extra £250 in reclaimed tax from the Inland Revenue.

And if the donor is a higher rate tax payer there's £150 tax relief for them on top - in other words 15% on the £1,000 sum bringing the total tax relief up to the full 40% .

In the period from October 1 1990 to February 28 1991 alone, tax of over £8 million on gifts totalling £26 million was repaid to charities!

It's expected that most of those who use the Gift Aid scheme will be people who have had a particularly good year financially but are unsure about the future and, therefore, their ability to continue to make charity contributions in later years.

That's why they would prefer to make a large one-off donation rather than commit themselves to regular giving through, say, a covenant.

VERSION A

Form of covenant by an *indivdual to* a *charity* for use *in England and Wales* from 31 July 1990

DEED OF COVENANT

NOTES

To_____ (Name of Charity)

I promise to pay you for _____years, or until I die if   **1**

earlier, such a sum as after deduction of income tax at the

basic rate amounts to £ _____   **2**

each [week] [month] [quarter] [year]   **3**

from [the date shown below] [_____]   **4**

Signed and delivered_____   **5**

Date_____

Full Name_____

Address _____

_____

Witnessed by:

Signed_____

Full Name_____

Address _____

_____

NOTES **1**. Enter the period of the covenant, which must be longer than *three years*. **2**. Enter the amount you will be paying to the charity. **3**. Delete as appropriate to show how often you will make the payment. **4**. Delete as appropriate. If you choose to enter an actual date *it must not be earlier than the date you sign the deed*. **5**. You must sign the form and enter the date you actually sign it in the presence of the witness who should also sign where shown.

VERSION B

Form of covenant by an *indivdual to* a *charity* for use *in Scotland.*

DEED OF COVENANT

NOTES

To_____ (Name of Charity)

I promise to pay you for _____years, or until I die if   **1**

earlier, such a sum as after deduction of income tax

at the basic rate amounts to £ _____   **2**

each [week] [month] [quarter] [year]   **3**

from [the date shown below] [_____]   **4**

Signed_____ Date_____   **5/6**

Full Name_____

Address _____

_____

Witnessed by: **6**

Signed_____Full Name_____

Address _____

and:

Signed_____Full Name_____

Address _____

NOTES: **1.** Enter the period of the covenant, which must be longer than *three* years. **2.** Enter the amount you will be paying to the charity. **3.** Delete as appropriate to show how often you will make the payment. **4.** Delete as appropriate. If you choose to enter an actual date *it must not be earlier than the date you sign the deed.* **5.** You must sign the form and enter the date you actually sign it in the presence of the witnesses, who should also sign where shown. **6.** In Scotland *two* witnesses are needed but, if you write the words 'adopted as holograph' above your signature, no witness is needed.

114

Chapter twelve

STAYING FIT
AND FEELING GOOD

It's never too late
to feel good

There is nothing any of us can do about growing older. But how and when it starts to notice is highly individual. Much depends on genetic inheritance, but even more on general fitness, too. Coupled with this come lifestyle and attitude.

Until recently it was assumed that as people got older they also became mentally less acute, physically weaker and emotionally depressed.

However, this has been shown to be very far from the case. The fact is the more you do, the more you can carry on doing! At the end of the day what matters is your attitude.

When you are at work you have a set routine and a network of friends and acquaintances in which you move. Status and position provide a valuable sense of identity and even if you aren't always in tip-top health, you simply haven't the time to dwell on any problems. The stimulation of work keeps you going.

The trouble is you lose all this the moment you retire, unless you replace the work routine with a whole new range of activities to compensate. That's why it's important not to underestimate the impact of retirement and to make sure that you are organised in advance with lots of new things to do.

Otherwise, before you know it, you could have got into the "happy doing nothing" lifestyle. The trouble is you probably won't be that happy and the less you do, the less you will want to do.

The secret is not to let this happen in the first place . . . if you plan well enough ahead you will go straight from one busy life into another potentially equally busy one.

GETTING USED TO EACH OTHER

You may have been married for years but the chances are you haven't spent all day and every day together for a very long time! So when you start looking at the future you need to work out a new lifestyle that will suit you both.

Think about retirement as a way of increasing your freedom of choice, giving you both the chance to make new friends, develop new interests and have a great time.

The chances are there are lots of things you talked about doing over the years but never had time for . . . and this could be the moment.

But it is important to give each other space. If yours is a "traditional" marriage where the husband has gone out to work while the wife stayed at home, a lot of adjustment could be necessary.

The husband who suddenly wants to take over the cooking, for instance, or who starts to question day-to-day household decisions after years of never being involved, could well upset a wife who has always been in charge on the domestic front.

The trouble is she will still have the same routine as she has always had - there will be the shopping to do, the cleaning and the washing. In other words, a wife in this situation may well not see herself as "retired" at all as her life will be just the same as before. And the danger is that real irritation can set in if this fact isn't appreciated.

So what's the solution? To plan for retirement together.

A husband who offers to help with the house as opposed to trying to take over running it, and a wife who becomes less rigid about just what has or hasn't to be done every day, are much more likely to have a happy retirement together.

That's why it pays to make time now to talk through how you see your retirement . . . then any problems can be ironed out before they actually happen.

KEEPING BUSY

It's a fact that the longer you carry on making maximum use of all your capabilities, from the muscles in your limbs to the memory-storing functions of your brain, then the more slowly you will age.

And this goes for both of you of course - so get out and find something to take up that you will both enjoy.

The trouble is there are lots of myths about retirement and if you don't find something to keep you fully occupied you can end up believing them.

There's the idea that you will need less sleep, for instance, as well the old wives' tale that growing older brings a lot more worry.

In fact, the amount of sleep you need is something that's particular to your own metabolism - if you can't sleep it could possibly be because your bedroom isn't airy enough! Or it could be that boredom has set in and you spend a lot of time nodding off in front of the TV during the evening. By the time you do finally go up to bed you have already had quite a lot of sleep and you are wide awake.

That certainly doesn't have anything to do with age - there are plenty of young executives who do exactly the same every night!

Worry has nothing to do with age either. Retirement itself can bring its own worries - most of which you can do something about. And it's certainly not worth worrying about those things you can't control.

Keep busy, keep interested and you will feel better for it. Set yourself a few challenges . . . vow to learn something new every day and you'll soon feel the benefit.

MAKING NEW FRIENDS

Like lots of people, if you rely on work for your social life you need to find other places where you can meet new friends in retirement. The best way is through an interest you already have - whether it's cooking, collecting stamps, playing bridge or joining an amateur dramatic society.

It's best, if you can, to go to places where there's a mixed age group - you don't just want to meet retired people. It's much more stimulating to meet a variety - if you are all the same age the danger is you end up wallowing in nostalgia as well as seeing everything from just one angle.

Don't rely too much on your own children to fill any gaps left by retirement. It may be great to see more of them now you are home all day, but don't spoil a good relationship with them and your grandchildren by relying on them too much.

The fact is your children have made their own lives, in which you obviously feature but can't expect to dominate.

Offers of extra babysitting may well be appreciated, but trying to make this your life's work would not be a good idea. For a start, babies have a habit of growing up fast and you could find yourself redundant before you know it.

WATCH WHAT YOU EAT

It's a fact that thin people live longer than fat ones - basically because there is less strain on their hearts. So if you are a little overweight, now is the time to lose a few pounds before it becomes a real problem.

Women in particular tend to put weight on as they grow older - their metabolic rate slows so they actually need fewer calories. But as we all know, it's all too easy to carry on eating as before.

There is no need to go on a starvation diet - a sensible eating plan should do the trick. But before you do anything have a word with your doctor first.

It may take a while to lose weight but if you eat sensibly then it should be a permanent loss. Cut out junk food and the empty calories like chocolate, cakes and biscuits and check you are getting enough fibre.

A sensible diet should contain the most important sources of each nutrient.

Every day see you have a serving of at least one of the following - lean meat, poultry, fish or eggs with green vegetables - cooked or in a salad - plus at least one root vegetable such as carrot.

Check your calcium levels - semi-skimmed milk has as much as full cream milk but is lower in fat if you are watching your weight. Yoghurt is also good.

Try pulses - kidney beans, lentils and so on - as an alternative to meat. Intake of red meat in particular should be watched - choose fish or chicken instead.

Don't be tempted, however, to cut down on the amount you drink - ageing kidneys cannot concentrate urine so well, so it is important to keep up your fluid intake, drinking at least three pints a day.

Alcohol, of course, should be taken in moderation.

And remember that many soft and canned drinks contain a lot of calories - try the low calorie versions of the most common ones for a change.

GETTING INTO SHAPE

Of course, being slimmer doesn't equal being fit. Taking up some exercise is the next step - but it is vital to have a check-up first.

It's just possible you could have a hidden medical condition and that embarking on an exercise programme could put you seriously at risk.

There are lots of simple things you can do around the house and garden that can help you get into shape. Experts rate digging the flower beds and mowing the lawn particularly highly in improving the three most important aspects of fitness - stamina, suppleness and strength.

Ordinary walking is great, too - leave the car whenever you can. A brisk walk with the dog is excellent exercise.

Check with your local authority about keep fit classes for your age group. Sports like swimming and golf are excellent - it's things like squash you should give a miss unless you have been playing for years and are confident you are fit enough.

CUT DOWN ON CHOLESTEROL

Much is said nowadays about cholesterol, a form of fat found in the blood and certain foods, notably eggs. It can clog the blood vessels, leading to heart and circulatory disease, like angina and coronary thrombosis.

Cholesterol levels can be tested with a free blood test at your GP's surgery. If the test shows that you have a high cholesterol level, a diet avoiding dairy and animal fats is likely to be recommended.

PRIVATE MEDICAL INSURANCE

If you're lucky enough to be covered by an employer's private medical insurance scheme while you're working, you'll have to consider whether you can afford to keep up the premiums yourself once you've retired.

As a rule premiums on private medical insurance increase as you grow older, even if you've been in the scheme for some time- it's a sore point that has been the subject of much controversy recently - and you may find the cost is too much to bear on a restricted retirement income.

It's worth shoppping around though, as there are now some special budget schemes designed especially for the over-60s.

Tax relief is available at either 25% or 40% - depending which rate the subscriber pays - for approved schemes, with relief given at the basic rate by deduction at source. Where relief is due at the higher rate, it is given by adjusting the subscriber's PAYE code. And if the premium is being paid for you by a relative or friend then they can claim the tax relief . . . at their top rate, too.

No smoking

If you smoke then the chances are that taking up exercise will leave you breathless and puffed out. It's been estimated that you shorten your life by five and a half minutes for every cigarette you smoke.

Yet despite all the overwhelming evidence that smoking is bad for you, more than 50,000 people still die each year from diseases related to cigarettes in Britain alone - the three main diseases relating to smoking are coronary heart disease, lung cancer and chronic bronchitis and emphysema.

Giving it up is a very positive step towards staying fit. For many people cigarettes are part of their routine. They light up at specific times of the day . . . at the morning coffee break, in the pub at lunchtime, for instance.

Retirement can give smokers the chance to break the habit because their routine changes.

When creating a new retirement lifestyle it's possible to design one that doesn't allow for cigarettes at all.

No-one is saying it's easy, but more than eight million people in Britain have managed it!

Most ex-smokers say the only way is to decide on a day on which you will definitely stop smoking, then throw away any cigarettes, lighters, ashtrays and so on. Try and identify the times when you are likely to miss a cigarette most of all - for lots of people it's after a meal or when they pick up the phone.

Then you can try to re-organise your life to avoid these situations making you weak willed.

You may find it helpful to give up with others - there are special groups all over the country you can join for support. Look out for ads in the local paper or ask your GP.

The stress factor

Lots of people smoke because they feel under stress. It's an increasingly common problem today and it doesn't just occur when people are working too hard.

It's quite possible to feel stressed even if you have very little to do and the best way to relieve stress is to deal with the problems and worries by facing up to them. Talking them through with a neighbour or close friend can help, but do get expert help if things are really getting on top of you. Your doctor should be able to help here.

Stress can also be reduced by getting involved in sport, a hobby or some other pastime. The enjoyment factor can help reduce the problem.

Lots of people don't believe it's possible to be stressed and retired at the same time but it most certainly is, especially for those who have given little or no thought to what to do now that work is finished.

That's when it becomes vital to find something else to fill the gap.

CHECK OUT YOUR HEALTH

Routine health checks for men and women are now available every three years, under the new NHS regulations. These checks involve measuring height, weight and blood pressure, together with an analysis of the urine and enquiries about smoking and drinking habits.

Similar checks are likely to be made if you register with a new doctor, and the over 75s should be offered more extensive annual checks, which can take place in their own homes.

In addition, a number of health centres now run "well woman" and "well man" clinics, as well as sessions to help those who want to stop smoking, take up exercise, etc.

Although no-one really enjoys a visit to the doctor, it's important that you take up the offer of these routine checks and attend any special clinics of relevance or interest to you - prevention is better than cure, after all.

The patient and doctor relationship is a partnership that deserves the input of both parties. By showing that you take an active interest in your health, you will, hopefully, get the best out of the partnership.

CHECKLIST

* One person's 60 is another person's 40. It's not your actual age that matters, but your attitude. Keep your mind alert by learning new things.

* Don't look ahead to retirement as an end. Instead plan for it by developing a second career or skill. Or try more education - the Open University can be the perfect starting point to learn all the things you have never had time to tackle in the past. And this will all help keep your brain ticking over nicely!

* Try something new . . . Glasgow, for instance, boasts a highly popular orchestra made up entirely of the "retired".

* Make a list before you retire of what you want to do. Include some exercise every day if you can and plan out a proper diet to follow. If you are home more, you might decide to have lunch as your main meal, for instance, and something lighter in the evening. Take a look in the library for healthy eating plans you can follow and devise a few of your own.

Chapter thirteen

GOOD SERVICE

Your rights as a consumer

Shopping is something we all do, usually without a second thought - until, that is, something goes wrong.

It's important to know your rights as a consumer. Then if something goes wrong, you'll know what to do about it.

Consumer rights are a subject of interest and relevance to all ages. But in retirement they are, perhaps, even more important than ever before - after all, you don't want to waste precious money on and be disappointed by purchases that don't work, break as soon as you've got them home or which are not what you expected them to be.

Your protection as a buyer lies in the Sale of Goods Act 1979, which covers all goods, including food, bought from a trader, whether from shops, street markets, doorstep salesmen, in sales, at parties in private homes, or by mail order.

It doesn't matter whether you pay for goods in cash or by credit - once the seller has accepted your offer to buy, a legally enforceable contract has been made which gives both of you rights and obligations.

Basically, goods must be:

* Of merchantable quality - they must be reasonably fit for their normal purpose, bearing in mind the price paid, the nature of the goods and how they were described.

* Fit for any particular purpose made known to the seller - if you ask for goods to perform in a certain way, and the seller assures you that they will, he has broken his contract with you if they don't.

* As described - for example on the package, display sign or by the seller.

If any of these obligations have not been met the seller has broken his contract with you and you may be entitled to your money back or compensation.

YOU ARE NOT ENTITLED TO ANYTHING IF

* You examined the item when you bought it, and should have seen the faults then.

* You were told about any fault - for instance, if the goods were described as "fire damaged".

* You ignored the seller's skill or judgement as to the suitability of goods for any particular purpose you described to him.

* You ignored the seller's claim that he wasn't expert enough to advise you correctly about your purchase.

* You simply changed your mind about wanting the article.

* You received the goods as a present - the buyer must make any claim.

WHAT TO DO

If there is a problem with goods you have bought, you should always complain to the seller, not to the manufacturer.

It is a good idea to examine and try out anything you buy as soon as you can. Once you have legally accepted goods which are faulty you lose your right to reject them and are no longer entitled to a full refund.

Acceptance normally means you have kept the goods beyond a reasonable time - you are expected to make it clear to a seller that you are rejecting goods as soon as possible after purchase.

WHAT YOU ARE ENTITLED TO

Provided you have not accepted faulty goods you do not have to accept a repair or replacement instead of cash compensation.

If you do accept a replacement or repair, write to the shop saying that you reserve your rights under the Sale of Goods Act to reject the goods - then you can ask for a refund if you are not happy with the repair or if further faults occur.

The shop may offer a credit note instead of a refund in exchange for faulty goods, but you do not have to accept one. Credit notes are sometimes valid for only a limited period and you may not find something else in that particular store that you want during that period.

Don't be put off by signs that say "no refunds without receipts" - they do not affect your legal rights and are, in fact, prohibited, so if you see one, tell your local Trading Standards Officer.

Don't be put off either by notices saying "no money refunded", even for sale goods - they are illegal and should also be reported.

GUARANTEES

A guarantee is always an addition to your legal rights under the Sale of Goods Act, so your rights are not affected when it runs out.

If you're asked to complete and return a guarantee registration card, it's a good idea to do so.

In theory a manufacturer could refuse to honour a guarantee if you did not return the card, though he is unlikely to do so if you have some proof of purchase, such as a receipt.

If a guarantee, or extended warranty, is being sold with the product, make sure you understand what is covered and what is not. Does the price justify the benefits provided?

SECONDHAND GOODS

Goods sold secondhand will probably not be in perfect condition, but they are still covered by the Sale of Goods Act.

Secondhand goods should still be of merchantable quality and fit for their purpose, but as with new goods, you can't complain about defects that were pointed out to you or which you should have seen.

If you're buying an expensive secondhand item, take someone with you to note what is said about it by the seller - in the case of cars, it's best to arrange an independent technical inspection before you agree to buy. At the very least, take someone knowledgeable with you if you don't know a great deal about cars yourself.

SALES

Sale items are covered by all the rules in the Sale of Goods Act - they must be of merchantable quality and perform the tasks for which they were made.

BUYING PRIVATELY

You have fewer rights when you buy something privately, whether it be from a friend, neighbour, or through a newspaper classified advertisement.

The Sale of Goods Act says that goods bought privately merely have to match their descriptions.

Your other rights will depend on what is said between you and the seller - what you were told about the value of the goods and their condition - so it is a good idea to take along someone who is knowledgeable about the item, or who could act as a witness.

BUYING AT HOME

More and more people now choose to avoid the hustle and bustle of the big shopping centres and shop instead in the comfort of their own homes. These days you can buy almost anything you want from catalogues, magazines or ordering by phone.

The Sale of Goods Act covers doorstep salesmen, "party" sales and other traders, and many firms who sell goods in your own home are members of the Direct Selling Association, which has its own code of practice.

Under the DSA code, "party" sales customers have 14 days in which to change their minds about goods ordered and get their deposits back. All sales leaflets must show the company's name and address.

Doorstep salesmen covered by the code must carry identification cards and company literature on the products or services offered. Customers also have 14 days to cancel agreements and claim full refunds on deposits.

BUYING FROM A DOORSTEP SALESMAN

Reputable companies, and those which are members of the Direct Selling Association, give their salesmen identity cards, so check he is who he says he is. If you're not interested in what he's offering, say "no thank you" and close the door.

* Beware of attempts to encourage you to buy in haste, such as one-off discounts or warnings that prices are about to rise. Ask for time to think things over.

* Find out what similar goods cost in the shops.

* If a doorstep salesman is trying to interest you in house repairs or improvements, get estimates of the cost from other firms.

* Never pay in full before receiving the goods or service. If you pay a deposit, insist on a receipt with the firm's name and address on it - and check they are who they say they are.

* Salesmen may make rash promises to get you to sign a contract, so if you want to order goods only on the condition that they are delivered by a certain time, make sure this is in writing.

* If you buy something from a doorstep salesman, keep the firm's name and adress in case of problems later.

* If you're buying on credit, make sure you know the full cost and compare it with other types of credit.

* If you sign a credit agreement in your own home, you have five days in which you can change your mind and cancel.

* You have the right to cancel contracts made during a doorstep visit even when no credit is involved, if a trader visits you without invitation or after making a phone call. In this case you will have a seven day "cooling off" period for cash contracts over £35.

BUYING BY PHONE

Phone sales are increasingly common - the caller will probably have got your name from the phone book or from one of several lists available to sales organisations.

Reputable companies should:

* Say who they are, and why they are calling.

* Phone you before 9pm.
* Ask if it is a convenient time.
* Not phone you at work.

If you are not interested, just say so and put down the phone.If you are interested, give yourself time to think the matter over and compare prices.

Don't give out your credit or charge card number over the phone if you have any doubts about the caller or the firm he claims to be phoning on behalf of.

BUYING BY POST

You have the same rights in law when you buy through mail order as when you buy from a shop.

If you buy from one of the large mail order companies which belongs to the Mail Order Traders' Association you are protected by a code of practice. The MOTA code provides for prompt delivery dates, the return of unwanted or faulty goods, servicing arrangements and a complaints procedure.

Check that delivery costs are included in the overall price when buying from a catalogue.

If you buy something from an advertisement, keep a copy of the advert plus details of your order, how you paid and the date on which you sent it. Never send cash through the post.

The Mail Order Protection Schemes and the British Code of Advertising Practice operated by the Advertising Standards Authority cover goods advertised from an advertisement, say in a magazine or newspaper.

The MOPS protect you if you send money for goods to an advertiser who goes into liquidation or bankruptcy before he sends the goods to you.

You have to apply to the Advertisement Manager of the publication which carried the advert within a specified time and you should then get your money back - publications which support a MOPS carry details about how to claim.

MOPS do not, however, cover classified advertisements or traders who advertise catalogues from which you have to order goods.

The BCAP requires mail order traders to deliver goods - except plants and made-to-measure items - within 28 days, or tell you if they cannot do so. They must promptly refund your money if you return unwanted goods undamaged within seven days, or if your goods are not delivered within 28 days and you decide you no longer want them.

WHO CAN HELP?

If you have a shopping problem and can't sort it out yourself, there are several agencies which may be able to help.

Trading Standards Officers investigate complaints and enforce laws relating to false or misleading descriptions of prices, inaccurate weights and measures and some aspects of the safety of goods.

Your local Trading Standards Department is listed in the phone book in the section for your local council, in Northern Ireland under the Department of Economic Development and in Scotland see the entry for your Regional or Island Council.

Often there will also be a consumer credit specialist at the Trading Standards Department, and Trading Standards officers have some responsibility for enforcing the law on some food matters, such as composition and labelling.

Consumer Advice Centres give a wide range of information and advice to shoppers and traders and their staff usually come under the wings of the Trading Standards Department too.

Environmental Health Departments enforce laws covering public health matters, like contaminated food and drink and dirty places where food is

stored, prepared and sold.

Their work also covers cleanliness in places used by consumers, such as hair salons.

Environmental Health Departments are listed in the phone book in the section for your local council.

There are around 1,000 Citizens Advice Bureaux which provide independent, free, confidential help and advice on a range of problems.

Some bureaux offer free legal advice and many will agree to act as "go between" in disputes between traders and consumers. They are listed in the phone book under Citizens Advice Bureau.

The Office of Fair Trading publishes a very useful set of leaflets, and the book Fair Deal, which explain consumer rights in more detail.

BUYING ON CREDIT

Buy now, pay later... it seems an attractive offer, and it's one made by all sorts of traders and companies nowadays.

But don't let offers of credit tempt you to buy something you can't afford. In most cases you'll pay much more than if you paid with cash, you'll be committing a chunk of your income for months or even years and, if you can't keep up the payments, you could find yourself in real trouble.

It's important, when buying anything on credit, to shop around for the best deal.

If you're being offered interest-free credit, remember to check the obvious - make sure the repayments don't add up to more than the cash price.

And look out for the APR, or Annual Percentage Rate, figures. If the APR is variable the interest rate and your payments can go up or down.

With that in mind, and if your retirement budget is tight, you may feel you'll be better off with a fixed interest loan where you pay the same amount each month.

When you ask for credit you'll be asked to fill in a form about yourself, your income and outgoings - answer these questions honestly.

You'll be doing yourself no favours, but will be breaking the law, if you make out that you're better off than you really are.

Once you've signed, you should get a copy of the agreement, and may receive another in the post. Keep it safely, together with a record of all the payments you make and copies of the statements you receive.

Credit offers often seem more attractive when you're in a shop surrounded by goods than when you're at home and able to take a realistic look at your financial situation. It may be that at a later date you wonder what you've let yourself in for and want to rid yourself of this sort of financial commitment.

But not all credit agreements can be cancelled - if you can cancel, there should be a box on the credit form which tells you about this option.

In the main, credit agreements can be cancelled if you met the trader to discuss the deal and signed the form at home.

If you signed in the trader's shop, office or other premises - like on an exhibition stand - you can't usually cancel.

Often people who have bought on credit get tired of being committed to monthly payments and make an effort to pay the balance before the agreement is officially due to end.

If you buy something on Hire Purchase, you can't usually end the agreement unless you're up to date with your payments, and you can't sell HP goods until the agreement has been paid off.

If you want to settle up a loan early, ask the company how much it will cost - you'll probably have to pay some of the interest you'd have paid if the agreement ran its full length.

In summary, buying on credit is a good idea only if you fully understand the agreement you are entering into and are sure that you'll be able to keep up with the repayments. In retirement it may be a good way to spread the cost of an expensive item, but don't overcommit yourself so there's no money left for the little luxuries you've been looking forward to all your working life.

And a final word of warning - if you act as a guarantor for somebody else's loan, you will have to pay all they owe if they stop paying. Don't be a guarantor unless you can afford to take that risk!

EXTRA PROTECTION

If you use your credit card to buy something costing more than £100, you usually have extra protection if something goes wrong.

If, for example, the hi-fi you bought won't work, or you spill paint all over the coat you've only had a couple of weeks, you may be able to claim from the credit card company's insurance scheme.

Most have a fairly generous time limit for such claims - usually around 100 days from the date of purchase. You'll need to supply proof of purchase, though, so make sure you keep copies of all the credit card transactions you make.

For more details, contact your credit card company direct.

LOST CARDS

If your credit card is lost or stolen, tell the company at once by telephone, then confirm it in writing.

It's vital that you act quickly in these circumstances. You won't be liable for the money spent if someone else uses your card after you've informed the company - but if it's used before then, you may have to pay up to £50.

The emergency numbers for the main credit card companies are as follows:

Access (Lloyds)	0702 338366
Access (Midland)	0702 352244
Access (NatWest)	0702 352255
American Express	071 222 9633
Barclaycard	0604 230230
Diners Club	0252 513500

Keep a note of your credit card numbers in a safe place, in case you ever need to report that they're missing.

Chapter fourteen

USEFUL INFORMATION

Up to date tax tables
and organisations to contact
for further information

TAX TABLES

PROPOSED INCOME TAX ALLOWANCES FOR 1991-92

Personal Allowance	3,295
Personal Allowance (age 65-74)★	4,020
Personal Allowance (age 75 and over)★	4,180
Married Couple's Allowance	1,720
Married Couple's Allowance (age 65-74)★	2,355
Married Couple's Allowance (age 75 and over)★	2,395
Additional Personal Allowance (for a single person who has responsibility for a child)	1,720
Widow's Bereavement Allowance (in the year of bereavement and the following year)	1,720
Blind Person's Relief	1,080
Income Limit for age-related allowances	13,500

★ These allowances are reduced if the taxpayer's income exceeds the income limit.

CHANGES IN PAYE CODES

Allowances	1990-91	1991-92	PAYE Code ends with letter	Increase in Code (x10 = increase in allowances)
Personal Allowance	3,005	3,295	L	29
Personal Allowance plus Married Couple's Allowance or Additional Personal Allowance	4,725	5,015	H	29
Personal Allowance (age 65-74)	3,670	4,020	P	35
Personal Allowance (age 75+)	3,820	4,180	T	36
Personal Allowance (65-74) plus Married Couple's Allowance (65-74)	5,815	6,375	V	56
Personal Allowance (age 75+) plus Married Couple's Allowance (age 75+)	6,005	6,575	T	57

INCOME TAX & NICs

SINGLE PEOPLE & MARRIED WOMEN UNDER 65

Weekly figures (£) - Income all earned

	Charge for 1990-91			Proposed charge for 1991-92			
Income	Tax	NICs	Net Income	Tax	NICs	Net Income	Cut in Tax & NICs
60	0.55	2.18	57.27	0.00	1.76	58.24	0.97
80	5.55	3.98	70.47	4.16	3.56	72.28	1.81
100	10.55	5.78	83.67	9.16	5.36	85.48	1.81
150	23.05	10.28	116.67	21.66	9.86	118.48	1.81
175	29.30	12.53	133.17	27.91	12.11	134.98	1.81
200	35.55	14.78	149.67	34.16	14.36	151.48	1.81
250	48.05	19.28	182.67	46.66	18.86	184.48	1.81
300	60.55	23.78	215.67	59.16	23.36	217.48	1.81
350	73.05	28.28	248.67	71.66	27.86	250.48	1.81
390	83.05	28.28	278.67	81.66	31.46	276.88	-1.79
400	85.55	28.28	286.17	84.16	31.46	284.38	-1.79
450	98.05	28.28	323.67	96.66	31.46	321.88	-1.79
500	117.17	28.28	354.55	109.16	31.46	359.38	4.83
600	157.17	28.28	414.55	146.29	31.46	422.25	7.70
700	197.17	28.28	474.55	186.29	31.46	482.25	7.70
800	237.17	28.28	534.55	226.29	31.46	542.25	7.70

INCOME TAX & NICs

MARRIED MEN UNDER 65

Weekly figures (£) - Income all earned

	Charge for 1990-91			**Proposed charge for 1991-92**			
Income	Tax	NICs	Net Income	Tax	NICs	Net Income	Cut in Tax & NICs
60	0.00	2.18	57.82	0.00	1.76	58.24	0.42
80	0.00	3.98	76.02	0.00	3.56	76.44	0.42
100	2.28	5.78	91.94	0.89	5.36	93.75	1.81
150	14.78	10.28	124.94	13.39	9.86	126.75	1.81
175	21.03	12.53	141.44	19.64	12.11	143.25	1.81
200	27.28	14.78	157.94	25.89	14.36	159.75	1.81
250	39.78	19.28	190.94	38.39	18.86	192.75	1.81
300	52.28	23.78	223.94	50.89	23.36	225.75	1.81
350	64.78	28.28	256.94	63.39	27.86	258.75	1.81
390	74.78	28.28	286.94	73.39	31.46	285.15	-1.79
400	77.28	28.28	294.44	75.89	31.46	292.65	-1.79
450	89.78	28.28	331.94	88.39	31.46	330.15	-1.79
500	103.94	28.28	367.78	100.89	31.46	367.65	-0.13
600	143.94	28.28	427.78	133.06	31.46	435.48	7.70
700	183.94	28.28	487.78	173.06	31.46	495.48	7.70
800	223.94	28.28	547.78	213.06	31.46	555.48	7.70

INCOME TAX: SINGLE PEOPLE & MARRIED WOMEN AGED 65-74

Annual figures (£)

Income	Charge for 1990-91	Proposed charge for 1991-92	Reduction in Tax & NICs
4,000	83	0	83
5,000	333	245	88
6,000	582	495	88
7,000	832	745	88
8,000	1,083	995	88
9,000	1,333	1,245	88
10,000	1,583	1,495	88
11,000	1,832	1,745	88
12,000	2,083	1,995	88
13,000	2,420	2,245	175
14,000	2,749	2,558	191
15,000	2,999	2,926	73

INCOME TAX: MARRIED MEN AGED 65-74

Annual figures (£)

Income	Charge for 1990-91	Proposed charge for 1991-92	Reduction in Tax & NICs
6,000	46	0	46
7,000	296	156	140
8,000	546	406	140
9,000	796	656	140
10,000	1,046	906	140
11,000	1,296	1,156	140
12,000	1,546	1,406	140
13,000	1,844	1,656	228
14,000	2,259	1,969	290
15,000	2,569	2,344	225

FOR MORE INFORMATION

Choice Publications Ltd,
Apex House, Oundle Road, Peterborough PE2 9NP. Tel: 0733 555123.

The Pre-Retirement Association,
Nodus Centre, University Campus, Guildford, Surrey, GU2 5RX.
Tel: 0483 39323.

Scottish Retirement Council,
Alexandra House, 204 Bath Street, Glasgow, G2 4HL.
Tel: 041 332 9427.

Occupational Pensions Advisory Service,
8a Bloomsbury Square, London, WC1A 2UA. Tel: 071 233 8080.

Pensions Ombudsman,
Michael Platt, c/o OPAS, address as above. Tel: 071 834 9144.

Inland Revenue,
Somerset House, Strand, London, WC2R 1LB. Tel: 071 438 6420

DSS Central Pensions Branch,
Newcastle upon Tyne, NE98 1YX. For a pensioner's identification card
BR464 - in place of a pension book, if you have your State pension paid
direct into your bank account.

DSS Records Division,
Special Section A, (101B), Newcastle upon Tyne, NE98 1YU. For help in
locating a missing pension fund.

IFA Promotion Ltd,
Information Office, 33 St John's Street, London EC1M 4AA.
Tel: 081 200 3000.

Securities and Investments Board,
Gavrelle House, 2-14 Bunhill Row, London EC1Y 8RA.
Tel: 071 638 1240.

Investor Compensation Scheme,
c/o Securities and Investments Board, as above.

Registry of Pension Schemes,
PO Box 1NN, Newcastle upon Tyne, NE99 1NN. Tel: 091 225 6393.

Office of Fair Trading,
Field House, Bream's Buildings, London EC4A 1PR. Tel: 071 242 2858.

The Law Society,
50 Chancery Lane, London WC2A 1SX. Tel: 071 242 1222.

The Law Society of Scotland,
26 Drumsheugh Gardens, Edinburgh EH3 7YR. Tel: 031 226 7411.

DSS Freephone,
Tel: 0800 666 555.

Association of British Insurers,
Aldermary House, Queen Street, London EC4. Tel: 071 248 4477.

British Bankers Association,
10 Lombard Street, London EC3B 9EL. Tel: 071 623 4001.

Building Societies Association,
3 Savile Row, London W1X 1AF. Tel: 071 437 0655.

Association of British Travel Agents,
55-57 Newman Street, London W1P 4AH. Tel: 071 637 2444.

Age Concern,
Astral House, 1268 London Road, SW16 4ER. Tel: 081 679 8000.

Help the Aged,
16-18 St James's Walk, London EC1R 0BE. Tel: 071 253 0253.

National Association of Citizens Advice Bureaux,
115-123 Pentonville Road, London N1 9LZ. Tel: 071 833 2181.